THE CONCORDE STORY

NEIL KELLY

MERCHANT BOOK COMPANY LIMITED

ACKNOWLEDGEMENTS

All the photographs for this book have been supplied by Adrian Meredith Photography except those acknowledged below. The publishers wish to thank Adrian Meredith Photography for their assistance in compiling this book and for the access to their unrivalled collection of Concorde photos. For more details of Adrian Meredith Photography please see back cover flap.

Other images courtesy of Ray Bonds: pages 9, 16, 17, 19, 20-21, 24, 31, 33 (top), 34-35. Corbis: page 107. Mike Bromfield: pages 61 (top left), 101 (bottom left), 103 (bottom), 104 (bottom), 117, 119, 120.121, 126-127 (centre), 130-131, 140-141, 147, 150-151 (bottom centre), 154-155. Arthur Gibson: pages 96-97, 152-153 (bottom). The Flight Collection: pages 76-77. Philip Jarrett: pages 22-23, 25, 26, 27, 28, 30, 32, 36-37, 42 (centre bottom), 43, 44-45, 47 (top right & Bottom), 48, 49, 50, 51 (top), 53, 55, 58-59, 60-61, 64-65, 66-67, 68, 69, 71, 72-73, 74, 75, 80-81 (bottom), 109, 111 (top right), 160. Robert Mathias: pages 11, 13, 14-15, 33 (bottom), 41. Press Association: pages 106-107,108, 118-119, 135, 162. David Wilson: page 165. © Steve Stibbens: pages 81, 82, 83.

Produced, designed and typeset by
Robert Mathias, Publishing Workshop.
Edited by: Ray Bonds

This edition published in 2005 by Merchant Book Company Limited
PO Box 10, West Molesey, Surrey, KT8 2WZ

ISBN 1 904779 05 0

Printed and bound in Singapore
by Stamford Press Pte Ltd

Contents

Introduction

Through the relatively short history of powered flight there have been many jaw-dropping events, but few can match the stunning impact of the appearance of Concorde – Britain's first supersonic airliner. The grace and beauty of this aircraft has amazed the world wherever it chanced to touch down. Each time it swept across the skies, observers have marvelled at its superb design and provocative style.

This book tells the story of Concorde's conception, her struggle for life, her survival against the odds and her premature demise.

This book is a tribute to a remarkable aircraft, her legendary and eventful career, and to the astounding achievement of the designers and engineers who made Concorde possible.

Chapter 1

Aviation Before Concorde

▼ It may have been just a 12-second hop covering a mere 120 feet, but when he accomplished it, on December 17, 1903, Orville Wright went into the record books as the first man to have flown a powered, heavier-than-air aircraft.
Inset: (L) Orville Wright and (R) Wilbur Wright.

December 17, 2003, witnessed a milestone in history. It was the centenary of controlled manned powered flight. The one hundred years prior to this date had almost certainly seen the most dramatic changes and advances in human technology since man first walked the Earth. During this period mankind developed into a species of 'flyers', achieving mass airborne passenger transportation, cheap and safe air travel, awesome airborne fighting platforms, men on the Moon and of course the subject of this book "supersonic passenger transport".

Following the first controlled manned flight by the Wright brothers it took just three years for powered flight to emerge from the 'Can it be done?' experimental stage to the point

where the question became, 'How can it be done better?'

Although man had taken to the skies before in balloons, gliders and a variety of powered machines, never before had he achieved the three key ingredients that define flying as we know it today. The three ingredients are, that the craft should be able to carry a man's weight into the air, the craft must be controllable by its pilot, and finally the craft must have a powerplant which can sustain it in level controlled flight: this is controlled manned powered flight. It was this achievement that set the Wright brothers apart from all of their aviation predecessors and was the true birth of aviation.

Once this milestone had been passed, the methodology and technology used to achieve it soon spread around the world. After the initial excitement of

the Wright brothers' famous flight in December 1903, interest in the USA quickly waned and the reality of turning the technology breakthrough into a reliable and practical form of transport began to dawn. Indeed, following several seasons of modest success with improving the Wright 'Flyer', the Wright brothers eventually returned to making their living by building bicycles.

Meanwhile, throughout the rest of the world and in particular Europe, a fair number of early aviators were following in the Wright brothers' footsteps, but more importantly advancing the development of more viable airplanes. The first recognised heavier-than-air flyer in Europe was Santos Dumont. He was no stranger to flying and had completed a string of successful projects, building dirigible airships driven by petrol engines.

In 1906, using parts from one of his dirigibles, Dumont constructed a box kite flying machine powered by a V8 petrol engine, and by 1909 he was building sophisticated monoplanes, including the 'Grasshopper' which could reach speeds in excess of 60mph. Indeed, he had the vision that other would-be flyers would pay to use his design and produced a number of Grasshoppers for sale to fledgling aviators, perhaps the world's first production aircraft. Another possible first for Santos was the construction of a test ramp on which to check out his aircraft before taking to the air, perhaps the world's first flight simulator.

By 1909, Louis Bleriot had flown across the English Channel. Another early aircraft constructor was British-born A. V. Roe. Having served an apprenticeship as a marine engineer, Roe, after hearing of the Wright

▲ Louis Bleriot piloted his flimsy No. XI monoplane, powered by a simple 25hp 3-cylinder Anzani engine, across the English Channel on July 25, 1909.

▲ *It was on July 12, 1910 that Charles Stewart Rolls, aviator and co-founder of Rolls-Royce, sadly became Britain's first aviation victim when he crashed his Wright biplane near Bournemouth.*

brothers' flight, turned his attention to building aeroplanes. He first flew in 1908 and by 1910 was producing aircraft, forming the first company to be registered as an aircraft manufacturer. Rather like Concorde production aircraft, Roe's designs were changing so rapidly in order to adopt new technology that few of his production aircraft were ever the same. In June 1909 Handley Page Ltd. became Great Britain's first publicly traded aircraft manufacturing corporation.

In England American-born Colonel S. F. Cody flew his biplane in January 1912, from Aldershot. The flight covered seven miles at an altitude of 70 to 80 feet, carrying four passengers. Despite this rapid development in heavier than air fixed-wing aeroplanes, in Europe hydrogen-filled airships were being developed to meet the demand for mass passenger air transport. Between 1910 and 1914, 25-seater Zeppelin airships were operating on scheduled services from Friedrichshafen on a round trip of German cities via Frankfurt, Potsdam and Gotha.

WAR IN THE AIR

In 1914 at the breakout of the First World War in Europe, aviation was predominantly a leisure sport with an emerging industry urgently designing and exploring new ways to improve performance and payload of aircraft in order to exploit aviation commercially. Until 1914, aviation was still coping with the startling realisation that man could finally get into the air and stay there. Not many people would have been too certain of the new flying machine's future potential; they were still struggling with trying to refine the basic concepts into more reliable and safer designs. Perhaps even fewer people had any visions that aircraft would be developed as a serious weapon of war, although Bleriot's crossing of the Channel had raised some blood pressure in various naval quarters. But by 1914 the A. V. Roe company had produced the Avro 504 fighter which saw out the war and was still in service with the RAF at the outbreak of the Second World War more than 20 years later.

It became very clear during the early stages of the First World War that observing the battlefield from aerial platforms above gave dramatic tactical advantages. Floating aloft in tethered balloons was a highly valuable asset but was limited in practicality, and highly dangerous. The balloons had to be on or behind your own lines; line of sight and range of view were limited, and the balloons were very vulnerable to attack. Soon the race for supremacy of airborne observation platforms began to elicit rapidly improving aircraft performance capabilities from the drawing boards. Aircraft had to be reliable, and have long endurance; they had to be fast to avoid gunfire from the ground, and manoeuvrable to avoid attack from enemy aircraft. As attack from the ground became less likely, pilots and designers accelerated aircraft development in a direction that focused on supremacy in air-to-air combat.

Hand-held weapons gave way to fixed machine guns as airborne fighting platforms became more sophisticated and far more lethal. The aerial 'dogfight' was born. It had always been a major goal in aviation to go faster with ever increasing control and manoeuvrability, but now the speed and agility of these fighting machines had become a matter of life and death.

In just four years of war and just 15 years after the first humans took to the air in controlled manned powered flight, military-driven development in aviation had produced literally hundreds of different fighter aircraft designs that could fly at speeds of 140mph, had endurance ranges of up to four hours, and could operate up to 20,000 feet. Hundreds of other designs emerged during this period, with a variety of light and heavy bombers achieving speeds of 115mph, operating at up to 20,000 feet and carrying payloads of up to 7,500lb of bombs on raids lasting up to seven hours' endurance. Engine development was driving performance; by 1918 engines were delivering 400 horsepower compared with the average 70 to 80 horsepower at the outbreak of war in 1914. Other types included reconnaissance and training aircraft, flying boats and seaplanes, while airship development carried on relentlessly, with Zeppelins that could cover 4,000 miles at over 70mph.

THE BIRTH OF COMMERCE

After the war ended, surpluses of heavy bombers and the need to reconstruct Europe's infrastructure quickly fuelled the birth of numerous peacetime aircraft operators and airlines. In 1919 six airlines were operating in France alone, covering the transport gap left by war-damaged surface transport infrastructures.

That year also saw the KLM airline formed. In 1919 the need to demonstrate the peacetime application of long-range aircraft prompted a proving flight by a Vickers Vimy from Hounslow Heath, near London, to Darwin, Australia, in 28 days. In America, Alcock and Brown flew the Atlantic non-stop from Newfoundland to Ireland, again in a Vickers Vimy. Also in 1919, airship designers were turning their attention to long-range passenger carriers as a British-built *R34* airship flew from the UK to New York. Passenger travel by air was less of an issue in the United States than in

▲ *On June 14th 1919 a converted Vickers Vimy bomber like that shown above, took off from Newfoundland to cross the Atlantic Ocean. Piloted by Captain John Alcock and Lieutenant Arthur Whitten Brown they flew 3043 kilometres in a little over 16 hours before they crossed the coast of Ireland.*

▲ *Years before London Heathrow became the major international airport it is today, it was nevertheless, a thriving and busy airfield.*

Customs were housed in a rather primitive tent (above), while (right) we can see an early version of a 'luxury' passenger lounge.

Europe. The USA had a highly developed, fast and comfortable railway infrastructure that had not been ravaged by war damage, and the focus of air transport was on fast mail delivery over long distances.

In November 1921 a joint Soviet-German enterprise, Deruluft, quickly opened a route between Kaliningrad and Moscow. Between 1923 and 1936, Dornier built great flying boats, with more than 250 rolling off the production lines and serving the South Atlantic routes. The later 1920s saw an

explosion in civil air transport. In 1923 Belgium's Sabena airlines was formed, while Britain's Imperial Airlines, Pan American and Japan Air Transport Company formed in 1924, 1927 and 1928, respectively.

In America, 1923 saw the first mail night flight from New York to Chicago, using ground based rotating beacons for navigation. Before too long the USA would have navigation beacons from coast to coast. The 1925 Kelly Air Mail Act deregulated air mail services, opening up the flood gates for multiple US air mail operators. By the mid-1920s aircraft construction was changing, with Germany and the USA building predominantly in all-metal construction, while France and Britain were still building in wood and fabric.

In 1927 Charles Lindburgh flew the Atlantic non-stop from west to east in his single-engined monoplane Spirit of St Louis. By the close of the decade the great Boeing aircraft manufacturer was beginning to stamp its authority on commercial aircraft design and production with the introduction of the first purpose-built passenger airliner, designed for comfort and practical route operations. The Boeing Model 81 could carry 18 passengers in spacious comfort at 140mph over distances of 450 miles.

In Europe the mighty Dornier Do-X carried more than 150 passengers and crew over 60 miles at a speed of around 100mph. It was powered by 12 engines in push-pull paired configuration and was at the time the world's largest, heaviest and most powerful aircraft. However, despite these impressive statistics it never entered production or scheduled service. In England the much smaller and commercially successful

Short Calcutta flying boat made its first flight in 1928, with a range of over 650 miles at 118mph on three engines.

By 1929, the shape of things to come was clearly forming. Just one year earlier, German airlines had carried a massive 10,000 commercial passengers, while American airlines carried 60,000 and the British and French following up with 27,000 and 22,000 passengers, respectively. However, in 1929 German airlines had increased their capacity to 120,000, while in America capacity more than doubled to a staggering total of 160,000 passengers.

THE ERA OF AIRSHIPS

Also in 1929, airships continued to mount their challenge on heavier than air machines. The German-built Graf Zeppelin completed a round the world trip in 21 days with a payload of more than 60 passengers and crew.

The 1930s saw commercial air travel beginning to come of age. In 1930 the Graf Zeppelin made a non-stop trip from Germany to Brazil. Between 1930 and 1937 the service would carry more

▼ Despite their immense size, the airships of the early days of aviation carried less passengers than today's state of the art airliner – Concorde.

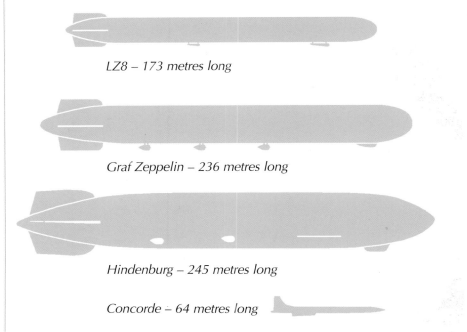

LZ8 – 173 metres long

Graf Zeppelin – 236 metres long

Hindenburg – 245 metres long

Concorde – 64 metres long

than a thousand passengers and tons of mail on this route, with the final leg of the journey being carried out by a Brazilian airline using fixed-wing aircraft. The passengers had berths during night flights, a restaurant, lounge, smoking room, bar and of course toilets.

British airship manufacturers pressed on also and in 1930 they produced the R101 which took to the air with cabin accommodation for more than 100 passengers and a dining room that could seat more than 50 diners at one sitting. However, on her inaugural flight she lost control in bad weather over France and crashed, killing nearly 50 passengers and crew. The R101 was withdrawn from service and Britain gave up on airships for passenger travel.

In Germany airship manufactures introduced the giant Hindenburg in 1936. More like a flying hotel and using modern aluminium alloys, the Hindenburg was kitted out in great

style, including an all-aluminium piano. It was capable of carrying nearly 200 passengers and crew.

However, in 1937 this aeronautical era came to a dramatic end when the Hindenburg as it approached its mooring mast near New York, burst into flames and crashed killing 36 people.

CONSOLIDATING AIR TRAVEL

In 1931, Imperial Airways introduced the Handley Page Hannibal, a four-engine biplane. Multi-course hot lunches and dinners were served to 40 passengers in superb soundproofed comfort.

From 1931 onwards the performance criteria for passenger aircraft began to reflect the staggering developments seen throughout the First World War. Aircraft manufacturers Junkers, Short, Handley Page, de Havilland, Boeing and Fokker, plus many more, were producing successful designs with

▼ The Handley Page HP42, introduced by Imperial Airways in 1931 provided a high level of luxury, reliability and safety seldom seen before in air travel. It went into service between London and Cape Town and the journey took an incredible 11 days.

increasing passenger payloads and speed while extending operating ranges to thousands of miles.

In 1932 two new names emerged; the Russian airline Aeroflot was formed, and a young Russian aircraft designer produced the ANT-20 Maxim Gorky, a monstrous eight-engined aircraft carrying up to 60 passengers. The young man's name was Andrei Tupolev. That year may also have seen the world's first low-cost, cheap-ticket airline. In direct competition with the established airlines, English motor coach operator Edward Hillman formed Hillman Airways, offering cut-price travel between Romford in Essex, England, and Paris.

In 1933 the American Boeing Corporation were fighting for market share with aircraft builder Douglas. First blood went to Douglas, whose airliner DC-1 met an airline design specification for a 14-seat commuter

airliner, beating the Boeing 247 that fell short of the required original design specification, carrying just 10 passengers in production configuration. This year also saw the creation of Air France, followed by Jersey Airways operating from the beach at St. Helier, while Italian aircraft manufacturer Savoia Marchetti introduced a 14-seat passenger airliner that cruised at 250mph, nearly 100mph faster than the Boeing and Douglas equivalents.

By 1934 even the British railway companies could see the revolution that air travel would bring to the world. With the help of Imperial Airways they formed Railway Air Services, operating a network of domestic services using de Havilland DH84, DH86 and DH89 aircraft. This was a very successful venture that continued operating its routes until it was consumed by the newly formed British European Airways in 1947.

Also in 1936, Britain's Short aircraft manufacturers introduced the Short S23 Empire flying boat, carrying 24 passengers on four engines at 165mph and with five hours' endurance. Imperial Airways brought into service nearly 40 Short C class flying boats to carry air mail around the Empire. These aircraft were the first to offer adjustable seats for passenger comfort on long journeys.

However, this period also heralded the beginning of a new era of flying machine, the flying boat. Floatplanes were already commonplace, particularly when operating in areas of the world where the provision of runways was not practical. Flying boats were considered to be safer on longer journeys over water, with the obvious belief that in an emergency they could put down

▶ *The North American F-100 Super Sabre was the first supersonic fighter to enter service. The 'Hun', as it was familiarly called, achieved super-sonic speed on the first flight of the prototype on May 25, 1953.*

on water. Few people considered that it would not be very safe trying to float a flying boat in the middle of the Atlantic in stormy heavy seas.

Another new breed of aircraft that emerged at this time was the Boeing 307. This aircraft introduced the world's first pressurised passenger airliner. The Boeing 307 Stratoliner, developed from the B-17 Flying Fortress bomber, had a pressurised cabin and could carry 33 passengers at 220mph above the weather at 15,000 feet, over a distance of 2,000 miles. The Boeing 307 first flew in 1938 and TWA (Trans World Airlines) put it into service on the transcontinental route in 1940, reducing the journey time to just over 13 hours, cutting two hours off the time taken by Douglas DC-3s.

The outbreak of war in Europe in 1939 affected civil aviation drastically. Despite the fast track input that military development would provide to aviation technology during the coming war years, many pre-war civilian airliner projects were delayed for five years and in some cases they disappeared altogether. Swissair became a casualty from the outset, having to halt civil

scheduled flying for the duration of the war. For some, though, 1939 was 'business as usual' as Pan AM opened up a new transatlantic route using Boeing 314 aircraft, each capable of carrying 84 passengers and crew.

As far back as 1933, German scientist Adolph Busemann was investigating the problems surrounding the increase in compressibility drag which would develop as an aircraft approached the speed of sound. Then, and for many years to follow, it was believed that this drag would increase to a point where at the speed of sound it would cancel the aircraft's, lift thereby imposing a physical limit to the speed at which an aircraft could fly.

In 1946, the Miles Aircraft Company was near to completion of comprehensive design plans to produce an aircraft that would fly at the speed of sound. Unfortunately, at this time there were large numbers of respected engineers who had reservations about overcoming the problems of supersonic flight. Similarly, others concluded that if supersonic flight were achievable then the limiting factor would be the pilots themselves. Supersonic flight would be

beyond the limits of human endurance, they argued, and dangerous to research. The Miles 52 supersonic design project was cancelled in favour of research into unmanned supersonic aircraft.

THE BIRTH OF THE JET AGE

In the 1950s the leading edge piston-powered passenger aircraft took 18 hours to cross the Atlantic; the race was now on for commercial jet passenger transport, and ultimately supersonic passenger transport, the SST.

So what is the sound barrier, what was this much-feared sonic boom and what are Mach numbers? In simple terms, the sound barrier is the speed at which an aircraft reaches and equals the speed of sound. The sonic boom is the sound generated by an aircraft as it exceeds the speed of sound and sends a shock wave ahead of it. Finally, and again simply, you can think of Mach 1

as the speed of sound. There are fine technical details that qualify all of the above definitions, but for a general understanding of supersonic flight they are all sufficient.

Throughout the 1950s, aircraft designers struggled with severe control problems and buffeting as higher and higher airspeeds imposed increasing stress on aeroplane wings. Designers learned early on that by sweeping back the wings of an aircraft they could reduce the stress and subsequent buffeting of the wings, allowing much higher subsonic speeds to be flown.

In 1953 The American-built F-100 Super Sabre fighter was the first aircraft to achieve Mach 1 in level flight. So rapid was the development of supersonic flight that just five years later, in 1958, the Lockheed F-104 Starfighter, once again American-built, was achieving in excess of Mach 2. When jet travel

▲ The Lockheed F-104 Starfighter was built in the 1950s to fly fast – Mach 2.2-plus at altitude. Often called 'the missile with a man in it', it had an incredibly small and thin unswept wing.

arrived the transatlantic journey time was cut to eight hours and now offered smooth passenger comfort at higher altitudes in rarefied air.

Between the wars the development of aircraft for peaceful commercial use was reborn and began to move on rapidly. Many people believed that there would never be another conflict like the Great War and were keen to pursue the pleasure of flight rather than develop its more murderous capabilities. However, many lessons had been learned and the holy grail of battlefield supremacy using airborne fighting machines was now well established. Alongside commercial aircraft development came a massive investment in military aviation projects.

As aviation began to blossom into the trendy sport and travel choice for the rich and famous, some countries, notably Germany, had secretly pushed ahead faster than any other nation with a range of aircraft types that would play a definitive role in launching attacks, delivering overwhelming logistics on the ground, winning the tactical battles and securing conquered territories. Hitler had planned well and at the start of the Second World War, the Germans had an air force equipped with fighters that could operate up to 30,000 feet with a range of nearly seven hundred miles, and at speeds in excess of 300mph. The German bombers were efficient weapons delivery platforms averaging 160mph over 750 miles with a lethal payload of 2,200lb. In Great Britain, on the other hand, although military aviation was moving forward, it was at a much slower pace in terms of innovation and production capacity. As an island nation, Britain's defence was still firmly

entrusted to a massive ocean-going fleet that was still considered to be the most powerful naval force in the world, the British Navy.

In contrast to the Luftwaffe, Britain's Royal Air Force lacked the numbers and quality of fighter aircraft that would be needed in the dogfights over Europe. The fastest British fighters were achieving only 230mph over 460 miles, albeit at a decent service ceiling of over 30,000 feet. RAF Bomber Command faired slightly better; its bombers' performance came closer to that of the Luftwaffe bombers, with figures of 150mph over 900 miles at 22,000 feet, carrying 2,800lb of bombs. The RAF also had two fast Hawker light bombers that could reach over 184mph but with much reduced bomb payloads of around 500lb.

In the USA the picture was much the same as that in Britain: fighters turning in more than 230mph over 600 miles at 27,000 feet, and bombers achieving much the same as their British counterparts, with the exception of the Douglas B-18A which had a speed of 225mph over 1,200 miles at 27,000 feet, with a bomb payload of 6,500lb.

As in the First World War, pilots and military strategists called for ever increasing speed and manoeuvrability in aircraft design, along with advanced and ever more deadly weapons systems. During this period of development, aircraft had become point and shoot weapons platforms that could perform close to the limits of aircraft controllability and the skill of the pilots who flew them.

Soon pilots of the Second World War were facing new roles to perform. Some designers were diverting their attention from aircraft speed and agility to a new branch of military aviation

development. The Germans had already come a long way down this road but now the ability to transport and deliver large payloads of bombs and equipment into enemy territory had become a critical strategic tool in the ever widening conflict. Once again, as a result of war, aviation was advancing rapidly on all fronts – speed, agility, payload, range and of course reliability. When the conflict ended in 1945, aviation had again reached extraordinary levels of advanced technical achievement, albeit at a terrible human cost.

Fighters could now fly at 485mph up to operational ceiling heights of 25,000 feet, and had extended ranges of up to 650 miles. Dramatic rates of climb and enhanced manoeuvrability and speed due to improved materials and increased horsepower from engines made the fighter of 1945 unrecognisable from those that had entered the conflict just six years previously in 1939. These statistics would have been even more dramatic had the war continued as both sides of the conflict began to introduce jet propulsion to their war machines.

Bombers could now deliver up to 22,000lb of ordinance deep into enemy territory on round trips of 1,660 miles, requiring nearly six hours of endurance both by day and by night. Mass movements of troops and equipment over long distances by air were now routine logistics in planning military campaigns, both offensive and defensive.

One further aviation legacy from the Second World War was the awakening of the giant American aviation potential. In the USA, development of commercial aviation applications had been more

▲ *The McDonnell Douglas F-4 Phantom had a wide-ranging and lengthy service career as a fighter, fighter-bomber, and recce platform. This is a US Air Force F-4G 'Wild Weasel' aircraft used for suppression of enemy air defences (SEAD).*

rapid than that of the rest of the world during pre-war years but military development had been relatively slower. World War II changed all that. From here on, American aircraft design would dominate nearly all aviation achievements for the next ten years, if not necessarily in technical innovation, certainly in production, deliverability and commercial viability, except in one key area, of course – and that is the subject for later chapters in this book.

Although the war years had attracted massive resources into aircraft design and huge advances in aircraft performance had been achieved, these achievements had come at a price. Due to the critical urgency for attaining aerial supremacy during the conflict, designers had been allowed to throw money, materials and fuel at their problems, with scant regard for commercial reality. The design criteria of the war years had always been focused on extra miles per hour coupled with any extra range and payload-carrying capability – and had to be deliverable 'next week'. Aircraft, though greatly advanced were generally too bulky, too heavy, too thirsty, and thereby in terms of cost and performance were not particularly well designed.

THROUGH THE SOUND BARRIER

The late 1940s and early 1950s heralded a new era in aviation development. The future and funding for both military and commercial aviation development was globally huge and well established. With a solid base of development and performance behind them, aircraft designers could now focus on designing for the longer term future rather than just for tomorrow. The goals remained largely the same – greater speed, payload

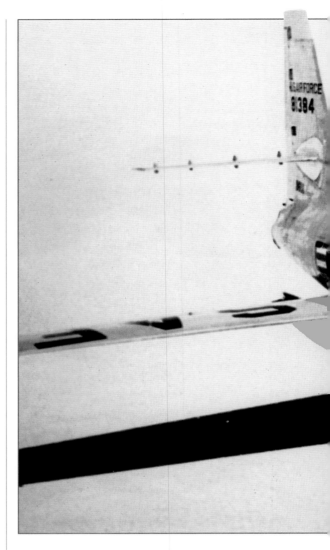

and endurance – but designers now had time to think about elegance in design and viability of improvements in performance and application of technology. This in turn led to a new wave of technical development, extending the horizons to potential performance enhancements that went way beyond the limits of the then current technology. It was now a case of dreaming up what you wanted to do and then develop the science and technology required to achieve the dream. Faint trumpeting that heralded the coming of the supersonic passenger transport age could clearly be heard.

On October 14, 1947, Chuck Yeager became the first man to break the sound barrier in the American-built

Bell X-1 jet plane. The Bell X-1 was slung underneath a Boeing B-29 Superfortress mother ship and carried aloft to 25,000 feet, which was the optimum height for the *X-1* to make its attempt to accelerate to beyond the speed of sound. For those on the ground the only view of the event would have been the X-1's vapour trail streaking ahead of the B-29. As he approached the speed of sound Yeager encountered the control problems that he and other pilots had met before as they probed the last few miles per hour close to the sound barrier. Severe turbulence rattled his eyes like beads in a child's rattle, but then Yeager's ride suddenly became smooth and quiet as the X-1 accelerated beyond the shock waves that were

pounding his aircraft. Observers on the ground heard a quiet distant boom; a few thought it was an explosion indicating failure of the attempt.

Soon after that ground-breaking event other manufacturers and countries were breaking the sound barrier also. In Britain, 1956 saw the Fairey Delta experimental aircraft setting a new world airspeed record of 1,130mph, now commonly referred to in Mach numbers as Mach 1.7.

In the commercial aviation world designers were focusing on maximum safety, improved reliability and increasing speed, but perhaps most of all was the Holy Grail of increased range and payloads at commercially viable operating costs. High aircraft development costs

▲ *The rocket-powered Bell X-1 was the first piloted aircraft to break through the sound barrier, and Charles 'Chuck' Yeager was the pilot who did it. On October 14, 1947 his aircraft was released from its sling beneath the belly of a Boeing B-29 Superfortress after which its own rocket powered away to achieve its phenominal speed.*

were now a 'given' and the aviation industry had adjusted to it, but the cost of operating the aircraft in airline service was becoming the key to full order books and individual aircraft success. Piston engine development was approaching its pinnacle of performance. Transatlantic passenger travel offering comfortable cabins and acceptable journey times while achieving good safety records had become available at commercially acceptable seat pricing. By now, air travel was beginning to remove middle class and business class travellers from the passenger lists of ocean-going transports. Travelling by sea as a first choice for 'getting to where you were going' was already heading for the history books. It still attracted heavy freight transportation and offered really cheap passenger carriage and, at the other end of the scale, spacious and luxurious travel. However, soon, enjoying the cruise as an item of choice on your travel itinerary would become the primary motive for crossing the Atlantic by sea.

By the close of the 1950s, the passenger airline industry had expanded dramatically on the back of relentless aviation technological advances. Scheduled services by a multiplicity of airlines to destinations all around the world were commonplace. In less than five decades since man had first taken to the air in properly controlled powered flight, aviation had changed the world so greatly both militarily and commercially that lifestyle at the turn of the century seemed more like 500 years ago rather than a mere 50. Mankind had truly begun to see no limits and was seriously looking to the stars and the possibility of passenger travel in space.

So what were the new challenges

facing aircraft designers? For fifty years they had been building bigger and more powerful engines, adding more engines, developing stronger and lighter materials that facilitated the construction of larger airframes with ever increasing payload capacity. So why not just carry on with a successful formula. Bigger engines mean more weight and more fuel. More engines mean more weight and more fuel. Larger airframes mean more drag, more weight and more fuel. The Bristol Brabazon, the famous aviation technical disaster,

proved the point – too big, too heavy and commercially non-viable. What was needed now was a major technology advance – smaller, lighter but more powerful powerplants providing more miles for less fuel, with a doubling in reliability. Airframes needed to be more streamlined and compact for higher speeds. The age of jet airliner passenger travel was arriving, not necessarily with the great trumpeting which accompanied earlier break-throughs, but more with an air of inevitability and foregone conclusion.

With the arrival in 1949 of the first passenger jet airliner, the British-built de Havilland Comet, the following 15 years saw new jet airliners taking to the skies at a breathtaking pace all around the world. But needed now were new, previously hard-to-imagine technical advances before a supersonic passenger aircraft could take to the skies. However, in the back rooms of several aircraft manufacturers, engineers were indeed 'imagining' what would need to be done in order to achieve those very same technical advances.. ▓

▼ On the 8th October, 1947, Britain's own pilot-less rocket-driven plane was launched from the belly of a Mosquito fighter-bomber over the Atlantic coast of Cornwall. The plane was piloted by Squadron Leader D. A. C. Hunt who was accompanied by Mr. C. B. Loche Bayne from the Royal Aircraft Establishment at Farnborough, Hants.

Chapter 2

The Plan to Build Concorde

▼ An English Electric Lightning F.3 of Royal Air Force 74 Squadron. The Lightning had a distinguished career as one of NATO's most potent combat aircraft of the 1970s. The aircraft's innovative wing design swept the wings further back into a 'delta' close to the fuselage as the speed increased to supersonic levels.

The list of requirements for the achievement of supersonic passenger transport was endless. Accelerated improvement in engine design, including radical new thinking on engine air intakes that would cope with scooping in air that was travelling at supersonic speeds. Brand new materials design, lighter than ever before, and revolutionary fabrication processes with sufficient strength to cope with the demand for super-thin and super-sleek airframe profiles. Such an aircraft would need to achieve a broader than ever range of flight and handling characteristics, with possibly the widest 'flight envelope' ever seen. To control these vastly different phases across this flight envelope would demand the latest control systems in order to make the aircraft flyable.

ENTER THE DELTA WING DESIGN

But perhaps the most significant hurdle

to overcome would be the super-thin delta wing construction that was now proven to be the optimum design for all aircraft flying faster than the speed of sound. Building such a large, finely sculpted delta wing would stretch airframe design construction to its limits and would require the invention of new construction materials.

Even during the closing stages of piston-engined military designs, swept wing and even delta wing technology had been used in long-range strategic bombers and experimental aircraft by both the Americans and the Soviet Union. Swept wings were more efficient at higher speeds and were featured on the draughtboards of most jet aircraft projects. However, if supersonic speeds were to be achieved then it was the stability aspects affecting wing performance in supersonic flight that had to be overcome. Swept wings would have to become much thinner

and far stronger while maintaining sufficient lift performance. This called for much lighter and stronger materials and new, more advanced manufacturing techniques.

With advances having been made in high speed jet fighter aircraft, the delta wing with its swept leading edge, larger wing area and thin section, would become the way forward for larger supersonic aircraft and many smaller fighters. Indeed, the delta wing design can be seen in Sweden's Saab and France's Mirage fighter designs, along with Britain's latest 'Eurofighter', or 'Typhoon' as it is now known.

Early delta wing experimental aircraft necessarily had very thick wing sections for strength, up to seven or eight feet thick. The construction resulted in heavy components and high drag coefficients, meaning that they were able to carry little or no useful payload. Before an aircraft could carry passengers at

▼ Another innovative early design – the British built Bristol 188.

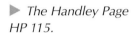
▲ The BAC 221.

► The Handley Page
HP 115.

more than the speed of sound, designers would have to develop materials and techniques to produce strong, thin-section swept wings.

The breakthrough came with the Fairey Delta prototype which first flew in 1954 and in 1956 broke the world speed record of 832mph with a new record speed of 1,132mph.

Another British aircraft, the Bristol 188, was developed primarily to carry out research and development trials aimed at solving the problems of kinetic heating. This is the generation of high temperatures in components used in the construction of large aircraft while flying at high supersonic speeds.

Whenever a new aircraft design is turned into a development project the extensive testing that is required is, to say the least, quite staggering. Most people would not be surprised at the

extent of airborne testing and measurement that is required before an aircraft enters service, but the level of testing on the ground before the aircraft can take to the sky is much more impressive.

TOWARDS CONCORDE

Concorde would be no exception and would encompass all of the traditional ground testing methodologies, plus a few unique to Concorde herself. Using design blueprints, a complete wooden 'mock up' of the aircraft is built. This model is accurate in every detail and is used to derive early indications of design and construction conflicts in the main airframe.

Separate test beds are built to test specific component parts of the aircraft. The engines are mounted on static frames and run at varying power settings for thousands of hours. Wing sections are encased in massive hydraulic rigs where loadings and flexing of the wings

are cycled again through thousands of hours in order to simulate the stresses that they will endure during many years of flight. The undercarriage is mounted in a huge lifting frame and loaded to simulate its share of the weight of the aircraft that it must support throughout the life of the airframe. The undercarriage is lifted and dropped

▲ A view from ahead of the long nose section of the full-scale wooden mock-up of Concorde.

◀ January 1968. The port main undercarriage assembly for the second prototype at the Filton Division of the British Aircraft Corporation. Trial installations and testing began immediately on arrival of the assembly from its French makers, Hispano Suiza.

would be subjected to ever increasing hydraulic loadings to find the stress fatigue limits. This airframe, located in Toulouse, France, was tested to destruction. The other airframe, housed at Farnborough, England, was fitted with a comprehensive air ducting system that could deliver hot and cold air throughout the airframe to simulate the dramatic and extreme temperature changes that the aircraft would need to withstand during transition between subsonic and supersonic flight, plus sustained high temperatures during the supersonic cruise. Yet another full size test bed of the aircraft fuel systems and fuel tanks had to be constructed on a three-axis hydraulic test rig in order to test the performance of fuel pumps and fuel transfer lines throughout all phases of flight, and in particular at high angles of attack during take off and landing.

STRETCHING THE LIMITS

Once again, in the case of Concorde, testing materials took on a whole new meaning. Development and testing of new materials for use in aircraft construction is and has been for years an ongoing process in its own right. But, in the case of Concorde, a far higher percentage of construction materials used would need to be 'new technology' so as to meet the higher design specification for flying such a large passenger jet at Mach 2. Brand new aluminium alloys had to be developed and tested for heat resistance and strength for use throughout the airframe and engines. In the end a copper based aluminium alloy, RR58, was chosen. Originally developed for the manufacture of gas turbine blades in jet engines, the material was now available in a wide range of profiles and sizes to

▲ A scale model of Concorde designed for use in the wind tunnel.

under load in "drop tests" which simulate landing loads. In addition to the above, test rigs were built for hydraulic systems, electrical generation and electrical distribution systems, flying controls and air conditioning.

During this testing of Concorde, new parameters had to be introduced into the ground test programme. In addition to the full scale wooden mock up, two nearly complete aircraft built from production materials were set up as structural test beds. One airframe suit all the construction requirements of Concorde.

To get the development going the visors on the prototype aircraft were aluminium, with crude cut outs giving limited forward vision to the pilots. Extensive testing on new glass technology would be needed to provide the fully glazed visor that would be required for aircraft certification.

New paint was required that could withstand the very high hull skin temperatures and tolerate the massive expansion of the skin area during supersonic flight. Wiring had to be developed to maintain integrity of the looms during the constant movement experienced throughout the flight as the airframe length increased and then decreased by up to 12 inches during every supersonic operation. In all, a wide range of new materials were developed and tested in addition to those mentioned above, including titanium, stainless steel, plastics, sealants, adhesives, and non-ferrous materials.

Despite Concorde's unquestionable advanced performance and innovative systems design, she was born in the 1960s and much of the flight deck instrumentation would be familiar to a relatively inexperienced private pilot. Concorde does not have an advanced 'glass cockpit' as is fitted in modern airliners. Most of the instruments are gyroscopic or electro-mechanical and include familiar items such as air speed indicator, artificial horizon, vertical speed indicator, distance measuring equipment, radio compass or ADF, horizontal situation indicator, auto-pilot and a standard compass. Even the engine condition indicators are mostly familiar, with exhaust gas temperature, fuel flow and pressures being displayed.

TECHNICAL DATA

Testing of the full-scale static Concorde test rig in Toulouse began in 1969; the objectives of the tests were to subject the airframe to operational design loads under varying operational temperature conditions.

Design loads were imposed on the airframe by 80 servo-controlled hydraulic jacks.

Kinetic heating of the airframe was achieved using 35,000 infrared lamps.

The data collection equipment could retrieve and process 4,000 data points every second.

Initially the airframe was cleared for a takeoff weight of 385,000lb. Over the following years further testing cleared the airframe takeoff weight to 400,000lb.

At RAE Farnborough the airframe test rig was shrouded in an 'oven glove', providing air ducting around the airframe; hot and cold air was circulated throughout the airframe to reproduce the cycling of temperature changes during operational flight.

Heating and cooling of the air was achieved by using hot water and liquid ammonia. Air was pushed around the system using five 2,300hp fans.

Loading of the airframe was imposed by 100 hydraulic jacks

The payload of a typical subsonic airliner is around 25 per cent of the total takeoff weight; in a supersonic airliner this payload is reduced to 7.5 per cent of takeoff weight.

Then there are a range of instruments that would be a little advanced for the rookie pilot but totally familiar, if not a little out of date, to any commercial pilot: double radio altimeters (essential on landing to the handling pilot who is nearly 40 feet above the tarmac as the nose wheel touches down); a computer controlled inertial navigation system which shows the position of the aircraft in latitude and longitude, plus other essential en route position data; and the traffic

▶ M. André Turcat, Sud-Aviation's Director of Flight Testing and the French Concorde's test pilot, seen here in the Concorde flight simulator cabin.

▼ A seemingly crude but effective steering control system devised for early use in the Concorde cockpit Simulator

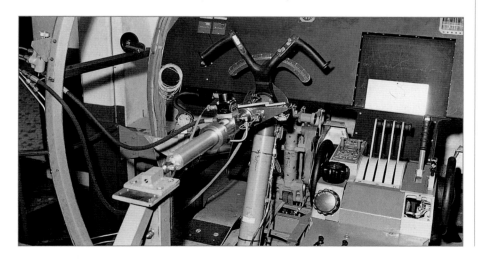

alert and collision avoidance system.

It would of course have been possible to retrofit Concorde with a modern 'glass cockpit', but this was not financially practical. Had Concorde stayed in production for a longer period, such instrumentation would inevitably have been fitted and certified as part of the ongoing development and production cycle; stand-by aircraft could have been used for retrofit certification. However, Air France and British Airways had only 13 aircraft between them, and these were in constant use on revenue-generating routes. As old as Concorde's cockpit was, it was best left alone.

Three systems that would have been alien to any non-Concorde pilots were the variable engine air intake controls and engine nozzle indicators, plus the centre of gravity meter and fuel transfer systems to move fuel between tanks in order to maintain a stable centre of gravity condition throughout the flight. On a conventional airliner this is normally compensated by trim tabs on the tail plane which slightly alter the angle of attack of the aircraft, thereby maintaining balance as the centre of gravity changes during flight. However, Concorde has no tail plane, and using trim tabs to maintain a compromised

A Royal Air Force Handley Page Victor B.1 'crescent' winged bomber – the last of the 'V ' bombers' to enter service, this one was photographed in 1957.

aerodynamic profile to the air flow would unacceptable at supersonic speeds. It is also important to note that Concorde does not have any high lift slats forward of the wing, or flaps on the trailing surface of the wing. Concorde does not have separate elevators and ailerons, rather 'elevons' which can be positioned in multiple configurations in order to perform the roles of the elevators and the ailerons during flight.

Despite Concorde's familiar look on the flight deck, there is much that would not be familiar when looking behind the controls and instruments at the underlying technology. Concorde was one of the first ever 'fly-by-wire' aircraft to go into production. The pilot's standard control yokes, rudder bars and other flying surface controls are not connected directly to the flying control surfaces themselves. Movement of the controls in the cockpit sends electrical signals, by wire, to hydraulic actuators adjacent to the elevons and rudder. However, fly-by-wire was in its infancy when Concorde was built, and a backup mechanical system was added in order to provide control in the event that both electrical systems failed. Because, during normal operations, the electrical system would not 'feed back' control surface resistance to movement to the cockpit flight controls, the pilot is denied the natural feel that enables him to apply measured control input. To compensate, artificial control surface resistance is generated in the hydraulic relays and fed back to the pilot via the cockpit controls.

Concorde has eight separate flying control surfaces, three elevons on each wing and a two-section rudder in the

▲ April 9th 1969 – Concorde 002, seen at Fairford after making her maiden flight from Filton, near Bristol. The photo clearly shows all of Concorde's eight separate flying control surfaces, three elevons on each wing and a two-section rudder in the fin.

fin. When all six elevons are positioned together in the upwards direction, they cause the aircraft to pitch up, and when they are positioned together in the downwards direction the aircraft will pitch down. When the elevons are positioned differentially (that is to say up on one wing and down on the other), they facilitate roll control, and have the same effect as a traditional aircraft's ailerons.

By mixing both of the above scenarios – for example, 10 degrees up on the starboard wing and 15 degrees up on the port wing, giving a differential with an up elevon bias – this results in a climbing turn to the left and vice versa for the reverse differential position. Positioning the elevons with a downward bias with differential positions facilitates descending turns to the left or to the right. On the flight deck the pilot can monitor the actual positions of the flying control surfaces and the integrity of the hydraulic

system serving them.

There are two hydraulic systems that are independent of each other, and each hydraulic system can be driven from any one of two engines. All four engines would need to fail in order to compromise both hydraulic systems. Despite this redundancy there is also a ram air turbine which can be deployed from beneath the port (left) wing during subsonic flight; when rotated by the air flow this will provide power to either of the two onboard hydraulic systems.

It was well understood from the outset that producing a suitable engine for supersonic transport would introduce a whole new chapter of new technology challenges and developments. Given the widely varying operating requirements of the engines when transitioning between subsonic and supersonic phases of flight, a new engine concept had to be introduced. The major components of the traditional jet engine would need to be separated out and developed indi-

vidually to meet the needs of supersonic flight. These main components would be the air intakes, the engine itself, the reheat system and the exhaust nozzles. Collectively, these four components would be dealt with as the Concorde powerplant rather than engine.

Dramatic development of the air intake system would need to be undertaken in order to enable the power-

▲ *TSR2 – the British Tactical Strike aircraft, became an inter-service and international political pawn before being cancelled by Britain's Labour government in the 1970s.*

◀ *A Vulcan bomber used as a flying test bed for the development of the Rolls Royce Olympus 593 – the eventual powerplant used in Concorde.*

TIMELINE

JUNE 1962

First discussions take place between French plane maker Sud Aviation and the British Aircraft Corporation (BAC) at BAC's headquarters in Weybridge, Surrey, and Paris.

European Space Research Organisation is born and one month later, and France grants independence to Algeria. In September Russia prepares to supply Cuba with missiles.

OCTOBER 1962

The British and French publish a specification for a supersonic airliner that will travel at twice the speed of sound.

Uganda gains independence within Commonwealth. Indian border positions attacked by China. Civil war in the Congo, and the Cuban missile crisis begins.

NOVEMBER 1962

A draft treaty is signed between Britain and France to build a supersonic passenger transport. The project will be shared equally between the two nations in terms of funding, design, manufacture and revenue from sales.

Ceasefire between the Chinese and Indian forces. United Kingdom in fresh talks with Europe over joining the EEC

plant to ingest rarified air at Mach 2 and reduce the air velocity to around 350mph for induction into the main engine stage. Within the engine component much higher temperatures would need to be handled compared with that in the engines on subsonic aircraft. For the first time, engine re-heat produced by injecting fuel into the engine exhaust would be included in a civil aircraft design, providing the additional power required for takeoff and for rapid transition from subsonic to supersonic flight.

In 1953 a Canberra aircraft, powered by two Olympus engines, broke the world altitude record. The Olympus engine was the obvious choice for Concorde. The basic engine was fully developed for subsonic use and was

already fitted to the Vulcan bombers, as well as to the early 'V bomber' contenders, the Valiant and the Victor now used for transport and airborne tanker duties by the RAF. In fact, early considerations for a viable SST included a Vulcan bomber converted to passenger-carrying configuration, giving a specification that would see 15 people travelling to New York in three hours at twice the speed of sound. Not surprisingly, the Vulcan bomber was used as a flying test bed for the subsequent development from the Olympus engine into the Olympus 593 powerplant used in Concorde.

The development of an Olympus supersonic powerplant had another

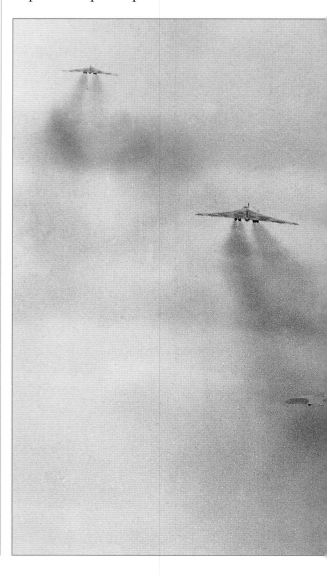

role to fulfil: though different to the Concorde specification, a supersonic engine designated the Olympus 302 was being developed for the new British military Tactical Strike and Reconnaissance aircraft, the TSR2. The TSR2 was scrapped by the British Labour government in 1965 but the supersonic Olympus 302 was the ideal choice for the ongoing Concorde programme. Over time the Olympus engine was developed from an original performance of 9,140lb of thrust to the current Olympus 593 that can turn in figures in excess of 40,000lb thrust.

In supersonic flight at Mach 2 air will enter the intake at about -60°C. From there it will be compressed and

TECHNICAL DATA

Although BAC held overall responsibility for the development of the Olympus 593, they only worked on the intake design. Rolls-Royce were responsible for the main jet engine. The exhaust nozzle was developed by French aero engine manufacturer SNECMA.

The Olympus engine used in Concorde was designed for the British 'V Bomber' requirement and saw service with the RAF fitted to the Vulcan bomber fleets.

The Olympus engine was upgraded for supersonic operation and fitted to the British-built TSR2 which was subsequently scrapped in favour of the American swing-wing F-111 fighter-bomber.

Later versions of the Olympus 593 have achieved a thrust of over 40,000lb. This is the equivalent of an 8,500,000cc petrol engine, or 10,000 small car engines.

When flying subsonic at high altitudes Concorde's skin temperature could be as low as -45 degrees Celsius; as speed increases the temperature rises to 0° Celsius at Mach 1, 120° Celsius at Mach 2, and would reach 300° Celsius at Mach 3.

Each Olympus 593 engine can burn up to 20 tonnes of aviation fuel per hour on full power settings with reheat.

slowed down to enter the main engine at 350mph and 130°C. By the time the air leaves the high-pressure compressor it will be at 550°C. Materials used in the Olympus 530 power plant are unrecognisable compared with those used in the original Olympus engine. The use of titanium reduces overall engine weight and provides higher protection against the ingestion of foreign materials into the powerplant intake.

In 1959 the initial specification to build a supersonic passenger transport was laid down. It would carry over 100 people from London to New York in just over three hours, travelling at more than twice the speed of sound 11 miles above the surface of the Earth. Just 30 years earlier, the pilots of passenger

◀ *Three Royal Air Force Vulcan bombers in line astern. The delta-winged Vulcan was one of the most successful aircraft of the post war years and was to prove an ideal test bed for Concorde.*

▲ The ground-breaking Sud-Aviation Caravelle with its rear mounted engines. This innovative French airliner was the first to adopt the principle of rear-mounted propulsion.

service aircraft carrying just eight to ten passengers at a speed of around 100mph sat in the elements outside of the passenger cabin and navigated their routes following railway lines. Just 26 years before this, controlled manned powered flight did not exist.

A EUROPEAN COMMITMENT

The requirement to develop new materials and technologies to facilitate the building of Concorde demanded such high numbers of skilled personnel that it proved to be too great for one European nation alone. In 1962, Britain and France signed an agreement to jointly develop and produce the Anglo-French Concorde. Some people in these design teams would spend over half of their working lives delivering Concorde into passenger service.

In 1956 the Royal Aircraft Establishment (RAE) at Farnborough set up a committee chaired by the Director of RAE and made up from members representing British aircraft and engine manufacturers, the airlines, and government ministries. The committee was called the Supersonic Transport Aircraft Committee, or STAC.

On the STAC committee was a Messerschmitt aircraft designer who had been spirited out of Germany after the war, along with several of his revolutionary Me 262 twin-jet-engined German fighters. Fortunately, these aircraft saw little action during the conflict as they arrived at the squadrons far too late and at a time when Germany had too few resources available to manufacture and fly them. The aircraft builder's name was Dietrich Kuchemann and he is credited with being the first to table the concept of a large, supersonic, delta wing passenger airliner.

In March 1959, the STAC announced recommendations to pursue two possible design concepts for SST. The first would carry 100 passengers over a distance of 1,500 miles at Mach 1.2, about 900mph.

The second, more ambitious design would have a longer range and higher speed, and be capable of carrying 150 passengers over 3,500 miles at Mach 1.8, well over 1,000mph. This second option defined the specification for transatlantic supersonic passenger travel.

After considering the STAC recommendations, Britain's Ministry of Aviation issued a number of contracts inviting manufacturers to produce designs for the larger transatlantic SST option. These first studies confirmed that the thin-section delta wing option pioneered in the early fifties would support stable control and efficient operation up to speeds in excess of Mach 2.

Fast wings were of no use unless they could support a viable passenger cabin to carry the payload. Two companies,

Hawker Siddeley Aviation and Bristol Aviation, were awarded a joint contract to determine the overall configuration of wings and passenger cabin design. Hawker examined the concept of having a large passenger cabin built into the centre section of a much thicker, swept flying wing. Thick flying wings had already been researched by the Americans at subsonic speeds using piston-engined powerplants. However, the more elegant thin wing and separate cabin option studied by Bristol was found to be the most viable of the two. The question now was how to build it.

In 1961 the newly formed British Aircraft Corporation (BAC) tabled a proposal to build an all-British design, the Bristol 223. This aircraft, powered by four Rolls-Royce Olympus engines, could carry 100 passengers and had a

▲ *The British prototype Concorde 002 at the engine testing bay at B.A.C.'s Filton Plant.*
  On this same day, September 12th 1968, the British Concorde was unveiled to the public for the first time.

range that would enable it to cross the Atlantic. The Bristol 223 design had superseded a previously cancelled Bristol 198, which would have carried 130 passengers across the Atlantic powered by six Rolls-Royce Olympus engines. However, the Bristol 198 involved design issues that were perceived to be beyond contemporary optimistic engineering expectations; it would probably have been too heavy, and have reduced payload. It would have needed the support of six thirsty Olympus engines, and the whole project would certainly have been uneconomic. Designers were becoming acutely aware of the fine balance between optimum aircraft efficiency and financial viability.

As a result of conditions in the contract imposed by the British government, BAC approached several possible collaborative partners from among aircraft builders in Germany, France and the USA. The Americans were busy considering their own SST options, and Germany at that time did not feel ready to get involved in such a costly and ambitious engineering project.

Only the French responded positively. As in the UK, the French aviation industry had been consolidated into a collaborative group similar to BAC, commonly described as Aérospatiale. Along with Dassault, Sud Aviation (who had built the ground-breaking, rear-engined Caravelle) were already working on medium-range SST concepts. Recognising the extraordinary technical programme that would be necessary in order to achieve transatlantic SST, the French favoured the medium-range development as a stepping stone towards full transatlantic capability. However, BAC recognised

that only the transatlantic and even longer-range options would capitalise on and sell the dramatic advantages of supersonic passenger travel, and therefore championed that design.

By now, both the French and British governments had been in direct ministerial contact regarding potential collaboration, and would soon announce their willingness to create an integrated Anglo-French SST development.

In 1962, at the Farnborough air show, BAC proudly presented to the world a model of their proposed SST. In October that year, the chief engineers of both BAC and Aérospatiale got together and produced full 3D design drawings for both the medium- and long-range SST concepts. These designs shared the same basic airframe but had different passenger cabin configu-

Concorde 002, the second of the two test prototype aircraft built, seen here arriving at Fairford Airfield in 1974.

rations and loadings to suit their respective operational requirements. Finally, on November 29, 1962, the British Government Supply Minister, Julian Amery, and French ambassador to the United Kingdom, Geoffroy de Courcel, signed the historic Anglo-French agreement to share the costs and rewards of developing and putting into service the transatlantic supersonic passenger transport soon to be named Concorde (with an 'e').

As BAC and Aérospatiale were already well into the design concept they were quickly able to define the respective roles for the French and British factories. The new aircraft would use modified British-built Rolls-Royce Olympus engines, which meant that the major responsibility for engine development would fall to the British.

To balance the situation, airframe development was weighted 60/40 in favour of French designers. The final major component responsibilities resulted in France developing the majority of the fuselage and the wings, while Britain would develop the engines, engine intakes, aircraft nose and tail section.

For efficiency in manufacture, the project would depend on seamless engineering collaboration that would allow discrete component parts to be manufactured in individual factories in France and the United Kingdom before being brought together on a final assembly line. Unlike the component manufacturing lines, there would be two final assembly factories, one in Filton near Bristol in the UK and the other at Toulouse in France. ▌

Chapter 3

Building Concorde

From the signing of the joint agreement it took just seven years for the first Concorde prototype to fly, in 1969. All in all over 500 British and French companies were involved in the building of Concorde.

Across the board it was necessary to develop brand new materials for the building of Concorde, and perhaps none was more important than the metal to be used in the majority of structural components. Extensive test-ing was carried out on titanium, aluminium and even stainless steel options. Eventually an aluminium alloy known as RR58 was selected for its all-round strength and good fatigue life when used in high load and high temperature operations. Nickel plate technology and components milled from solid blocks of titanium were used for high temperature hotspots in the newly redesigned Olympus engines. New welding techniques were

▶ *Because of Concorde's steep angle of attack during take-off and landing, the variable positioned 'Droop Snoot' nose was designed and developed to allow its pilots better visibility.*

Developed from the Boeing 377 Stratocruiser (left), it is not difficult to see how the strangely proportioned hybrid transport aircraft (below), nicknamed 'Guppy', got its name.

developed using electron beams.

For many years, full scale wooden mock-ups of aircraft were built during the development phase to ensure that all parts actually fitted together before finally approving engineering drawings to be used in producing highly expensive metal components. Concorde was no exception: a full scale wooden model was built, including detail such as engines, engine mountings, the famous (fully working) 'droop snoot' and even the specially designed variable air intakes for the Olympus engines, all precisely produced according to design drawings, and all in wood.

The aircraft would be built in two different locations, Filton in the UK and Toulouse in France. With Britain producing the nose, tail, forward parts of the fuselage and the engines, while the French factory produced the wings and the centre section of the fuselage, it would be necessary to transport large components between the two factories. A special aircraft was built for the task: the new 'Guppy' was based on the Boeing Model 377 Stratocruiser airliner, with a hold capacity of over 30 tons in payload and 1,100 cubic metres in volume. (Aero Spacelines' Super Guppy 201 registration F-BTGV can be seen in static display at Bruntingthorpe in Leicestershire.)

In addition to the logistical problems of moving these large components it was essential that parts made in different factories would be engineered to the highest possible standards of accuracy. The engineering drawings used by the builders in Toulouse were identical to those used by British engineers in Filton. Furthermore, designers and engineers from both countries would have to learn each other's languages.

The first prototype, 001, was French-built; the second, 002, being rolled out at Filton in Avon.

As the first British and French prototypes of Concorde took to the air, in America a long-running debate on whether to enter the race to supersonic passenger flying was still unresolved. However, President Richard Nixon announced that his government would approve funds to invite designs for a US-built Supersonic Passenger

TIMELINE

September 1965
The British Aircraft Corporation begins the construction of the first Concorde airframe at its factory at Filton, near Bristol.

Following race riots in California the previous month, American students take to the streets protesting over American involvement in Vietnam. Late this year Ian Smith announces Rhodesian Unilateral Declaration of Independence.

▶ *The enormous Olympus 593 turbojet engines jointly manufactured by the Bristol Engine Division of Rolls-Royce Ltd and the French engine company, SNECMA.*

▼ BELOW: *February 6th, 1968 – work progresses on prototype Concorde 002 in the Brabazon Hangar at Filton.*
BOTTOM: *The following Easter Concorde 002 gets a coat of paint in the red, white and blue livery of BAC/SUD.*

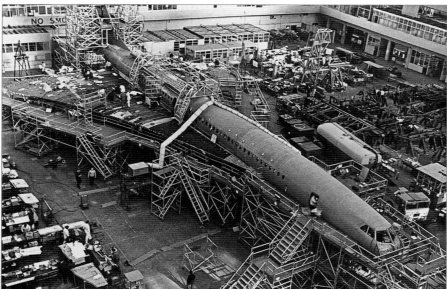

TIMELINE

April 1966

With the French companies running a schedule slightly ahead of that of the British, the first French prototype Concorde 001 moves to the final assembly lines in Toulouse.

Two months earlier, Freddie Laker starts cut-price transatlantic airline, Laker Airways. Australia joins the fighting in Vietnam, and British hovercraft invention begins scheduled ferry services across the English Channel.

August 1966

Four months behind the French schedule, British Aircraft Corporation begin the final assembly of the first British prototype, Concorde 002.

Work on the Olympus engine presses ahead as Rolls-Royce carry out air tests of the engine by fitting it to the underside of a Royal Air Force delta wing Vulcan bomber.

The previous month the England football team beat West Germany to win the World Cup. Francis Chichester begins solo circumnavigation of the globe in his yacht. Later this year, 147 school children are killed in Wales as a colliery waste tip buries their school.

Transport (SST). The specification demanded that the aircraft would fly at 1,700mph, with a prototype flying in 1972 followed by entry into passenger service in 1978.

THE OPPOSITION

Boeing Aircraft Corporation won the design contract and unveiled plans for the Boeing B2707 (see page 46). At 318 feet long this aircraft would be the

largest supersonic passenger aircraft ever built to that time and would carry over 300 passengers at a speed in excess of the design specification of 1,700mph. The project proved to be too ambitious, however: with swing-wing design and built from titanium, the components required to support such a large aircraft would have been too heavy and too costly. The project was cancelled in 1971.

On the other side of the world the Soviet Union had been building their own SST, the Tupolev Tu-144 (see page 47). Very similar in looks to Concorde, it was duly nicknamed 'Concordski'. With a design specification slightly better than that of Concorde, it would carry 121 passengers at Mach 2.3 over a distance of 4,000 miles. The Tu-144 actually made its maiden flight two months ahead of Concorde's, on

▲ September 12th, 1968. Concorde 002 prototype at the engine testing bay at the British Aircraft Corporation's Filton plant. On the day this photograph was taken the airliner was unveiled to the public .

TECHNICAL DATA

Concorde rotates (takes off) at an angle of 13 degrees up to the horizontal and takeoff speed is 217 knots. In the climb she pitches up to 20 degrees and maintains 250 knots at a climb rate of 4,000 feet per minute, then she reduces her pitch angle to 12 degrees and climbs away at 1,200 feet per minute.

Concorde main fuselage dimensions:
Overall length 202 feet 4 inches (61.66m)
Length from tip of the nose to the cockpit 24 feet (7.31m)
Height from the ground to the top of the fin 40 feet (12.2m)
Maximum external width of fuselage 9 feet 5 inches (2.88m)
Maximum internal width of cabin 103.4 feet (2.63m)

Maximum internal cabin height 77 feet (1.96m)
Cabin length (flight deck door to rear bulkhead) 129 feet (39.32m)
Concorde wing dimensions:
Wingspan 83 feet 10 inches (25.6m)
Wing length 90 feet 9 inches (27.66m)
Wing area 3,856sq. ft (358.25sq. m)

Concorde tail fin dimentions:
Height 37 feet 1 inches (11.32m)
Length 34 feet 8 inches (10.58m)
Area 365sq. ft (33.91sq. m)
Rudder area 112sq. ft (10.41sq. m)

▶ *Concorde assembly progress at the Toulouse St Martin facility of Aerospatiale. In the foreground are sections of aircraft N0. 9, while in the background, and almost finished, is aircraft No. 1.*

▲ A mock-up of the Boeing Corporation's giant B2707. It stretched an incredible 318 feet long. It would have been the largest supersonic passenger aircraft ever built up to that time and would have carried over 300 passengers at a speed in excess of 1,700mph.

▶ A view of the Boeing B2707 from the rear, showing the enormous power unit .

December 3, 1968.

With Captain. André Turcat in command, Jaques Guiraud as co-pilot and engineers Henri Perrier and Michel Petif, Concorde 001 made her short maiden flight on March 2, 1969. Just over a month later Brian Trubshaw was at the controls of Concorde 002, accompanied by co-pilot Brian Watts. On this occasion he was taking British-built 002 on her maiden flight from Filton near Bristol to Fairford RAF base in Gloucestershire. RAF Fairford was considered a more suitable airfield from which to base the Concorde test programme due to the availability of a

▲ The incredible length of the giant Boeing B2707 mock-up under construction.

▼ The Soviet airliner Tupolev Tu-144, aptly nicknamed 'Concordski', waits on the runway prior to its maiden flight.

TIMELINE

January 1963
President Charles de Gaulle of France refers to the planned supersonic passenger transport as 'Concorde'.

President de Gaulle blocks Britain's admission to the EEC. One month later the Russians agree to bring their troops home from Cuba. In June of this year France withdraws her navy from NATO. In August over one million pounds is stolen in the 'Great Train Robbery'.

October 1963
In Britain, the press are being treated to views of the first experimental models of 'Concord'. (At this stage the British were not spelling Concord with an 'e'.)

French singer Edith Piaf dies; the USA signs treaty to control nuclear weapons testing. The following month President John F. Kennedy is assassinated in Dallas, Texas.

May 1964
A British built experimental supersonic aircraft, the BAC 221, is test flown by the makers, British Aircraft Corporation. Ironically, the test flights are conducted in the south of France to take advantage of the better weather.

Earlier this year France and Britain agree to build a Channel tunnel; the Greeks and Turks fight in Cyprus. In June Nelson Mandela goes to prison in South Africa.

November 1964
In Britain, the recently elected Labour government unveils its plan to pull out of the agreement to build 'Concord'.

Lyndon B. Johnson becomes president of the United States of America. The following month, the British parliament votes to end capital punishment.

January 1965
The Labour government is forced into a 'U turn' and announces that Britain will continue to participate in the 'Concorde' project after all.

Winston Churchill dies and is given a massive state funeral. Throughout the year America becomes ever more embroiled in Vietnam, and a Russian becomes the first man to leave his spacecraft for a 'space walk'.

longer runway and relatively high security arrangements. Later that year, both Concorde prototypes, 001 and 002, appeared at the Paris Air Show together.

TESTING FOR SERVICE

During the following seven years of test flying, prototype Concorde 002 clocked up over 800 flying hours, becoming the most tested civil aircraft in aviation history. However, she never saw passenger service and, after a brief spell in a French museum , 002 was flown to Yeovilton Royal Navy Air Museum in Devon and remains there on static display today. In March 1977, captained by Brian Trubshaw and John Cochrane as 1st officer, Concorde 101 (pre-production aircraft) made her last flight into Duxford airfield in Cambridgeshire where she takes pride of place in the British Aircraft Collection among a variety of other famous British aircraft.

In October 1969 Concorde 001 (F-WTSS) was the first Concorde to

break the sound barrier, followed by Concorde 002 (G-BSST) in March 1970. Flying twice as high as Mount Everest at speeds in excess of the muzzle velocity of a rifle bullet meant that flight operations for Concorde included many new and sophisticated techniques not seen in previous jet airliners. They covered the broad flight envelope from high thrust reheat takeoffs through high altitude cruising in rarefied air on the edge of space, to low speed handling required for safe approach and landing.

Concorde flight controls included many new automated systems to assist the pilot. Thus, conversion from conventional jet liners to Concorde was designed to be completed in relatively few hours' flying time. During the flight-testing phase, many airline pilots were invited to fly the prototypes, confirming that Concorde was definitely a

◀ *March 2nd, 1969 – Concorde 001 makes its maiden flight from its base at Toulouse, France piloted by André Turcat (above centre).*

▲ *Concorde test pilots André Turcat, France and Brian Trubshaw, Britain talking with the press after piloting Concordes 001 and 002 to Paris in1969 (below), – the first time the planes had appeared together*

▶ *Concorde 001 proved a firm favourite with French enthusiasts at the Paris Air Show.*

▶ *The huge engine nacelles of Concorde 001 housing the Olympus 593 turbojets .*

◀ Test instrumentation on board Concorde for gathering in-flight data.

▼ In-cabin speed display.

pilot-friendly aircraft.

Kinetic heating caused by air friction at high speeds raised temperatures in Concorde components to in excess of 100 degrees Centigrade.

Later in the flight testing programme Concorde engineers conducted test researching in the Earth's upper atmosphere, including any potential effects caused by Concorde itself. It was found that Concorde's condensation or vapour trail consisted of almost pure water. Contamination of the high atmosphere by Concorde's four Rolls-Royce Olympus engines proved to be minimal.

The Concorde design team planned for 4,000 test flight hours. During the test flights, computers and flight data recorders gathered detailed information

TECHNICAL DATA

Normal operation speed limits:
Maximum operating cruise speed Mach 2.04 (1,350mph)
Maximum permissible range 4,500 miles or 3,900 nautical miles
Takeoff speed 250mph   Landing speed 185mph
Maximum landing gear extension speed 270kt
Maximum visor-down extension speed 325kt
Maximum speed with nose down 5 degrees 325kt
Maximum speed with nose down 12.5 degrees 270kt
Maximum speed for landing light extension 270kt
Maximum speed for windscreen wiper operation 325kt
Maximum positive incidence (angle of attack) 16.5°
Maximum operating altitude 60,000 feet

Temperature and pressure limits:
Maximum total temperature on the nose 127° Celsius
Maximum oil temp for start and takeoff 125° Celsius
Maximum oil temp during continuous operation 190°

Celsius
Minimum oil pressure during continuous operation 5psi
Minimum oil pressure for takeoff 10psi
Minimum fuel temp for start up -40 degrees Celsius
Maximum fuel temp during continuous operation 50° Celsius

Weight limits:
Max weight without fuel (zero fuel weight) 203,000lb (92,080kg)
Operating weight empty 173,500lb (78,700kg)
Max payload 29,500lb (13,380kg)
Max takeoff weight 408,000lb (185,000kg)
Max taxiing weight 412,000lb (186,880kg)
Max landing weight 245,000lb (111,130kg)
Max weight of fuel 26,400 gallons, 210,500lb (95,680kg)
Max baggage weight 14,570lb (6,622kg)

TECHNICAL DATA

Passenger payload:
Maximum number of passengers certified as 128
Normal number of passengers in single class cabin layouts:
British Airways 100; Air France 92
Flight crew, 3 – captain, co-pilot and flight engineer
Maximum flight attendants, 6
Escape exits, 6 with escape slides – 2 main front, 2 over wing centre and 2 at rear.
Passenger toilet facilities, 3
Crew galley facilities, 2
Passenger information displays, 2 displaying Mach number, air speed, outside temp and distance to destination
Baggage holds combined volume, 697cu. ft. (20.3cu.m)

Engine specifications:
Engine model Olympus 593 Mrk610 turbojet, number fitted four
Engine manufacturer Rolls-Royce/SNECMA
Maximum thrust produced at takeoff, per engine, 38,050lb (170KN) (with afterburner reheat in operation)
Maximum thrust produced during supersonic cruse, per engine, 10,000lb (4,536kg)
Performance enhancement due to reheat, 20% at full thrust during takeoff
Fuel, Type A1 Jet fuel
Fuel capacity 26,400 gallons /119,500ltrs/95,680 kg
Fuel consumption (at idle power) 1,100kg/hr (302 gallons/hr)
Fuel consumption (at full power) 10,500kg/hr (2,885 gallons/hr)
Fuel consumption (at full re-heated power) 22,500kg/hr (6,180 gallons/hr)
Typical miles to the gallon per passenger 17 miles!

▶ *The normal complement for cockpit flight crew is three – a captain, co-pilot and flight engineer.*

on every aspect of the flight. However, even this was not enough and the entire crew, particularly the pilots, would be thoroughly debriefed verbally after every flight, with engineers gath-

ering vital information not detected by the surveillance electronics.

September 1973 saw the fastest-ever transatlantic crossing by a commercial passenger aircraft. The flight landed at Orly airport in the Southern Paris suburbs after a flight of three hours and thirty-three minutes from Washington Dulles airport.

Concorde was not just brand-new technology; the design teams had embarked upon a project to produce a Supersonic Passenger Transport. This was not an experimental project: it was the real thing. Much of the technology that would make Concorde fly had only been tested on paper, a risk normally associated with research and development projects. It was crucial that prototypes 001 and 002 should move quickly through early stages of the test programme to prove that the project was viable and that all the planned new technology would in fact work. The designers were crucially aware that these early prototypes had to perform close to specification, not only to support the concept of the aircraft, but because this aircraft was committed to going into service and would need to be viable in airline operations. As unthinkable as failure and cancellation was, it would be better to know earlier than later if the development plan had to be revised.

Perhaps not surprisingly, the designers had done their homework well. Despite the totally new handling characteristics required and a flight profile never before seen in a commercial airliner, the designers had planned the control and flight systems perfectly. Pilots flying the early prototypes found that, with careful attention to the training required to master the new han-

dling techniques, Concorde 'did what it said on the box'. This fact was a tremendous boost to the flight test programme. The development team could focus on performance and refinement with far less attention being needed on basic handling and pilot training. This was to be a useful and financially favourable characteristic of Concorde when the time came to convert existing airline pilots onto the new Concorde fleet.

Many people are surprised to learn how soon the two first prototypes were retired and how relatively few flying hours they clocked up between them. However, when one considers that in a more rational development programme, given the totally new technology concepts that had to be proven, they would have been classed as 'proof of concept' and 'experimental'. They were in fact quite unique in aircraft development terms – that is to say, they were probably too advanced to be called experi-

mental but not close enough to final operational specification to be considered as pre-production.

So the pre-production aircraft, Concorde 101 and 102, sometimes referred to as 01 and 02, were built by the French and British teams, respectively. Throughout the whole Concorde programme, French aircraft were planned to roll off the production lines some months ahead of their British counterparts. This was graphically evident in the final versions that became 101 and 102. Given that so much new ground had to be broken and that this would take much longer than most aircraft development programmes, it was always expected that the pre-production models would be quite significantly different to their prototype predecessors, 001 and 002.

By the time that 101 and 102 took to the air much had changed. The Olympus 593 had been substantially tested and modified on test beds, and a

▲ July 1st, 1972 – the British prototype Concorde 002 arrives back at London Heathrow Airport after a successful overseas sales tour.

TIMELINE

February 1967
The sales campaign continues as airlines are invited to view a fully fitted mock-up of what the interior of Concorde will look like in production.

During the previous month three American astronauts are killed in a fire during a rehearsal on the Apollo launch pad. US action in Vietnam increases to new high levels.

May 1967
More than 15 airlines around the world have placed options for a total of 74 Concorde airliners. Things are looking good.

Muhammad Ali, formerly Cassius Clay, is charged with evading being drafted into the American army. The following month Egypt, Syria and Jordan invade Israel, the Israelis strike back and in six days Israel had routed all three invading armies and captured large areas of Arab lands bordering Israel.

December 1967
In Toulouse French Concorde prototype 001 is rolled out of the hangars for the first time for the first full public viewing. Anthony Wedgewood Benn (British Minister for Technology) announced that Britain would adopt the French spelling of Concorde, with an 'e'.

Just one month earlier, Charles de Gaulle once again voted against Britain joining the EEC.

brand new air intake system had been designed to cope with the extraordinary task of operating conventional jet engines in the rarefied air close to the edge of space. In actual fact, the short gap between the completion of 101 and 102 meant that the new air intake systems on these two aircraft were quite different, with 102 enjoying a specification that closely matched that of the final production aircraft. The pre-production models had different wing sections to those of the prototypes and could now carry the fuel payload that would be necessary in order for Concorde to deliver a practical passenger payload across the Atlantic.

The pre-production aircraft flew even fewer hours than the prototypes; in fact, the prototypes had been so successful that much of the developments that might have been anticipated in the pre-production programme had already been dealt with on 001 and 002. Concorde 101 and, more specifically, Concorde 102 simply took the achievements of the prototype programme and smoothly transformed them into a production specification.

THE REAL COSTS

Despite the success of the early prototype aircraft and their successors, the pre-production aircraft, this Concorde production programme was now operating in an ever more hostile environment. The world outside was changing faster than ever before. The whole Concorde design concept was already on the edge of what could technically be achieved at that point in time. Add to this the tumultuous political environment of the day and the now-massive commercial pressure on all of the world's product markets, Concorde still had a way to go.

'Production' aircraft 201 and 202 would never see significant passenger service, and each of them flew few more hours than their pre-production predecessors and the original prototypes. However, the aircraft did extensive test flying in support of the modifications that would be required to bring Concorde up to full operational specification and secure the vital Certificate of Airworthiness. Their role became that of honing Concorde into superb pinnacle of aviation technology. Aérospatiale and British Aerospace had delivered a practical and viable Supersonic Passenger Transport that

would meet and surpass all of her original design specifications.

Originally, the costs budgeted for developing the supersonic transport concept amounted to less than £100 million. How wrong could they possibly be? Although the British and French aircraft manufacturers had years of experience which should have enabled them to accurately assess development costs, they were about to embark into unknown aircraft design territory and had completely miscalculated the full extent of the ground-breaking new technologies that were going to be required. Behind the scenes, this cavalier assessment of the development budget was aided and abetted by both the British and French governments, who had their own agendas for pushing ahead with the project.

As well as becoming the world's most remarkable aviation achievement, and remains so to this day, Concorde also had a hand in Britain's political direction towards the close of the 20th century. In addition to the unquestionable advantages in partnering with French aircraft manufacturers in the building of Concorde, it is almost certain that some of the weight behind the decision to sign the Anglo-French accord was to help win support from General de Gaulle and gain his vote

▲ *One of the two nacelles of the prototype Concorde 001 equipped with two Olympus 593 engines. The SNECMA exhaust system can be seen in the foreground.*

agreeing to admit Britain into the European Common Market. The French were sceptical regarding Britain's intentions in participating in the Common Market and a project like this could only help to dispel Britain's 'go it alone' image in France and throughout the rest of Europe.

The French aviation industry was warming to the idea of a joint venture since French engine technology was far behind that of Rolls-Royce in Britain. Getting access to the Rolls-Royce Olympus engines was essential in order to put their Supersonic Transport ambitions into practice. However, in January 1963, just two months after signing the Anglo-French accord and the contract to build Concorde, General de Gaulle announced that France would exercise its veto to block Britain's entry into the Common Market 'at this time'. However, during the same public statement, de Gaulle confirmed that the Anglo-French agreement to build Concorde remained solid and would be pursued to completion. This was the first time that the Supersonic Transport project was referred to as *Concorde*, with an 'e', in public.

Unquestionably, the escalating cost of building Concorde had more than just a little to do with the way in which the project was managed from the start. From a political standpoint, the decision to split responsibility, obligation, costs and reward on a fifty/fifty basis between the two participating nations was a reasonably sound idea, in particular concerning a deal between the British and the French. However, from a business management perspective it generated ever increasing compromises, delays and costs.

Senior management teams were rotated between French and British personnel about every two years. By the time the incoming managers had got their feet under the table and over-turned what they did not like about the outgoing regime's decisions, getting on with the job and progressing the project during their two years in office would be considerably curtailed. Add to this the fact that procurement managers would have to put the nationality of prospective contractors at the head of the procurement criteria, depending on which part of the programme was

▲ *Concorde Delta-Golf awaits the OK to take-off from Fairford – 1974.*

being fulfilled, and it can be realised that it was not always possible to select the best and most cost effective tenders from potential contractors.

Senior BAC managers were later to make the claim that the bureaucratic regime imposed by the original agreement and contract could have added as much as 50 per cent to the final bill for Concorde's development.

In summary, the true cost of building Concorde had never been properly budgeted; the project was partially driven by political motivation, and at the outset both governments embarked on the venture with the intention of 'footing the bill' whatever the cost.

Just as politics helped to nurture Concorde into life and provided the 'life blood' of near unlimited funding, in 1964 Britain's new Labour government hatched a political plot to kill Concorde off. With a huge deficit in Britain's finances and a bag full of expensive promises to the British electorate, Chancellor George Brown needed a massive cash injection from somewhere and had his eyes set on the USA as a donor. The plan was simple: Britain would cancel its funding of

▶ *December 3, 1967 –*
Toulouse. A noseless
prototype Concorde 001
crosses the Blagnac aero-
drome on its way from the
Blagnac workshops to the
St Martin plant.

TIMELINE

February 1968
Concorde's
Olympus engines go
into production with
a massive advance
of cash from the
British government.

Kenyan Asians start
arriving in Britain
fleeing from perse-
cution in Kenya.
The following
month the world's
largest aircraft the
Lockheed C-5
Galaxy is unveiled
in the USA.

During this summer,
Uri Gagarin, the
first man to go into
space, is killed in an
air accident, Martin
Luther King and
Robert Kennedy are
assassinated, and
decimal currency is
launched in the
United Kingdom.

some large expensive capital projects,
say in aerospace, namely TSR2 (see
page 33), the English Electric
Lightning fighter (see page 24) and,
'oh yes', Concorde. This would open
the floodgates for the American aerospace industry and give them access to
huge aerospace contract opportunities,
and in return, they would lend Britain
the cash to bail out the UK economy.

By this time the English Electric
Lightning was almost fully developed
and well into the late stages of it's
flight-testing programme. Cancelling
this project on purely financial grounds
was not a particularly wise decision
since the majority of the Lightning's
development costs had already been
spent. However, Roy Jenkins, Minister
of Aviation, had already decided that
the future of high speed supersonic
combat fighter aircraft was in
unmanned remotely controlled supersonic platforms and that funding
should be withdrawn from piloted
supersonic fighter projects. It is
rumoured that test programme results
concealed performance data on the
Lightning in order to keep it in the
subsonic domain, thereby avoiding the
automatic cut for manned supersonic
fighters. Thankfully, the Lightning
survived and went into service with the
Royal Air Force. It had an illustrious
career as one of the world's two most
successful interceptors of the time, the
other being the McDonnell Douglas
F-4 Phantom (see page 19).

TSR2 was not to be so lucky. It was
in a much earlier stage of development,
with outstanding new technology
requirements as yet unresolved, and
therefore required much more ongoing
funding than the Lightning. Across the
Atlantic, the General Dynamics F-111

swing-wing tactical fighter-bomber was
deemed to be 'nearing completion and
ready for service'. The F-111 was built
to serve a similar combat role to that of
the TSR2; it was on offer to Britain at
a price anticipated to be far lower than
the route of completing TSR2 development. Furthermore, the Royal Navy,
who wanted government funding to be
diverted from TSR2 into a project to
upgrade the now ageing Blackburn
Buccaneer, were in Australia lobbying
the Australian government to cancel its
options on TSR2 and call for upgraded

TIMELINE

August 1968
French prototype 001 begins taxi trials in Toulouse.

The first British prototype Concorde 002 is rolled out from its hangar at Filton. At the same time, Britain's first pre production aircraft, Concorde 01, is nearing completion.

Ronald Reagan announces that he will run for president as Russian tanks spearhead a swift and dramatic invasion of Czechoslovakia.

December 1968
On New Year's Eve 1968 the Russian-built Tupolev Tu-144 supersonic transport 'Concordski' makes its maiden flight. Nikita Kruschev fulfils his dream as the Soviet Union beats the rest of the world in the race to be the first to fly a supersonic passenger transport.

One week before, on Christmas Eve, American space ship Apollo 8 took three men to the Moon and carried out 10 orbits before returning to Earth.

Buccaneers, which they duly did.

All of these and perhaps other less well documented circumstances brought down the axe on TSR2. History now shows that TSR2 was indeed far superior to its American counterpart, the F-111. Furthermore, delays in final development meant that the F-111 was delivered late and way over budget, at subsequent cost to Britain. Other than satisfying a short-term cash flow problem for Britain, the cancellation of TSR2 simply took money from the British aerospace industry and gave it straight to the American airplane builders.

So how did Concorde escape this relentless cull of innovative British-driven aviation projects? The Labour government of 1964 had definitely made the decision to scrap funding the development of Concorde. However, they had seriously misunderstood the French response to their plans and, ironically, due to its mistrust of the French, had previously compromised its position in the drafting of the original Anglo-French agreement.

The French government would not agree to the cancellation of Concorde; nor would they take over complete control and responsibility for the project. Finally and categorically, the French would not consider the possibility of any other nation becoming involved in the Concorde project, in particular the United States of America. The basis for this firm stance by the French government was buried in the detail, or should we say lack of detail, in the original contract. When the original agreement was drawn up, the British mistrusted the French government's resolve to see the project through to completion. Somehow, the British had succeeded in finalising the contract having left out any options for participant nations to withdraw from the project, and that included Britain. In or out, Britain was going to have to pay 50 per cent of the development budget come what may. Reluctantly, the British government had to back down and continue its support and funding for the Concorde project. Concorde had survived the cull, and this outcome would prove to serve the aircraft well during her following 40-year career.

In 1963, once again political agendas were about to play a significant part in Concorde's future – only this time, it was American politics that introduced a threat to Concorde in the form of a serious competitor to the Anglo-French supersonic transport dream. Having made his now-famous speech in 1961 committing the United States to putting a man on the Moon by the end of the decade, President John F. Kennedy was pumping millions of dollars into the NASA space programme in order to fulfil his dream and his promise to

the American people. Kennedy made it clear that the Moon mission was the top aerospace project in the USA, and unusually allowed the race to produce the world's first supersonic passenger airliner to be relegated to the 'nice to have' category, even to the point where America would accept not coming first. Given that the Americans were beginning to dominate aviation around the world, perhaps they felt that only they would achieve commercial success in supersonic passenger travel, and being first was not the Holy Grail.

So things would have remained had not the bosses of Pan American

Airlines stepped into the ring. In June 1963 Pan American Airlines had placed options on no fewer than six of the European-built supersonic transports. No doubt this was never intended to be a real option to buy the planes: for a few thousand dollars and a guaranteed leak to the American press Pan Am achieved their objective. President Kennedy rose up again and delivered yet another dramatic promise to the American people. Kennedy committed his administration to support the development of the world's first, biggest and best supersonic passenger airliner. Furthermore, this project was

now moved to the top of his political agenda and the US treasury would need to prepare to spend the money that this project would demand.

Boeing were at the forefront of the development plans and produced a stunning and potentially innovative solution to the SST project. In the end, Boeing were to spend over one billion dollars on the Boeing 2707-200 project (see page 46) without ever completing a single prototype. President Kennedy's SST never took to the skies, and as a result America's ambitions to join the supersonic passenger airliner club was formally cancelled. ■

▲ Concorde prototype 001 penetrates the nylon barrier of the Hispano-Suiza arresting system for the second time during testing. Penetration here has reached as far as the aircraft's main landing gear.

Chapter 4

Selling Concorde

With the first orders or options being placed in June 1963 by British Overseas Aircraft Corporation (BOAC), Air France and Pan American Airways, the Concorde order book swelled rapidly over the following couple of years and reached a total of more than 70 orders or options placed by the mid-1960s. Interest in Concorde had been committed to the order books by 17 airlines from 10 countries and four continents around the world, with a massive 44 aircraft being earmarked by North American airlines alone. At this

point hopes must have been high that Concorde was destined to be a world-wide commercial success, overcoming the now growing costs of development.

In 1971, ahead of the much publicised British Concorde tour of the Far East, the French campaign to sell Concorde took 001, now registered F-WTSS, on a sales tour to South America. This was the first transatlantic crossing by Concorde 001. After landing in Brazil she stayed for two weeks, appearing at shows and giving demonstration flights.

Ahead of a 'round the world' flight demonstration tour, the marketing campaign began focusing on the startling fact that, now, no two airports in the world were more tan 15 hours flight time apart.

The world tour took Concorde to the Middle East, where Iran placed an order for two Concordes, then to the Far East via India, during which Singapore, more commonly known as a relaxing stop-over, faced the reality that developing and achieving fast turnaround techniques on the ground could make Singapore a vital hub in the world of supersonic travel. The final legs of the tour took Concorde to Tokyo, then on to Sydney, Australia.

Throughout the tour, Concorde was greeted by hundreds of thousands of spectators who flocked to the airports in order to witness the spectacular sight as she approached at an extraordinarily high angle of attack, looking more like a huge bird of prey swooping

▲ *1968 – An early visualisation of Concorde in BOAC livery.*

◄ *A clear view of the 'Droop Snoot' nose in take-off position. For landing the nose is lowered much further.*

TIMELINE

March 1969
Just over two months behind the Russian Tu-144, French proto-type Concorde 001 makes its maiden flight from the runway at the Toulouse manufacturing plant in the south of France.

The previous month, the Boeing 747 made its maiden flight, and the Americans sent the Mariner 6 space probe to Mars. Chinese troops are fighting again, this time on the border with the Soviet Union. In the UK, all BOAC flights are grounded due to a strike by pilots.

April 1969
British built prototype Concorde 002 makes her maiden flight from Filton. At the end of this flight Concorde 002 is repositioned at RAF Fairford in Gloucestershire, where the longer runway will provide a more suitable base during Concorde's initial test flight programme.

France withdraws from NATO and President de Gaulle resigns. In the UK the QE2 departs on her maiden voyage.

Later this summer Neil Armstrong becomes the first man to step foot on the Moon, British troops are deployed on the streets of Northern Ireland, Colonel Gadaffi comes to power in Libya, and colour television comes to Britain.

October 1969
Concorde 001 exceeds Mach 1 for the first time.

P & O liners cease sailing to India.

to the ground. Once on the ground, Concorde would taxi majestically among conventional airliners. Not since the introduction of the de Havilland Comet had a single airliner stood out so much from the crowd. But this was now on a much grander scale. No one could have known that Concorde would parade in this way for the rest of her flying career, without a single challenge to her supremacy both on the tarmac as well as in the air.

Expectations regarding Concorde's potential order book were high, with an anticipated production run of 200 aircraft. The mood was that all major airlines would have to have Concorde in their fleet, such was the unique and prestigious reputation of the aircraft. However, in the end just 74 original options would be the total to be placed, and just 20 aircraft were eventually built for two airlines alone, the British and French national carriers, British Airways (formerly BOAC) and Air France.

By the time of the Paris Air Show in 1973, newsreels around the world had

been regularly documenting Concorde's progress towards scheduled and anticipated routine supersonic passenger air travel. The world was in awe of the technological advances, and there were few or no doubts about the inevitable success of SST.

At the Paris show, Concorde was joined by the other contender for SST, the Russian-built Tu-144, for all the world looking like a clone of Concorde herself. 'Concordski' was about to stun the world with a totally unexpected and spectacular crash in front of a global audience. Not since the mid-1950s had the public witnessed such a disaster at an international air show.

The Tu-144 had been modified with retractable forward canard wings, and the engine configuration had been updated, providing more space between the two engines on each of the wings. Concordski would seek to emulate the now familiar and dramatic display given by Concord.

The true cause of the crash has never been published, but speculation suggests that the Tu-144 pilot was forced

▲ *The Russian built Tu-144, looking a little too 'suspiciously' like its rival Concorde – and aptly nicknamed 'Concordski'.*

▲ British prototype Concorde 002 after a day's extensive testing at Fairford.

to carry out an unscheduled steep climb followed by a dive to avoid potential conflict with another aircraft in the air in the vicinity of the show. This theory suggests that the violent avoiding manoeuvre exceeded the design loadings for the Tu-144 and she literally broke up in flight, first losing a wing, followed by multiple structural failures.

As well as the six crew on board the aircraft, a further eight people were killed on the ground as the wreckage fell over a wide area north west of Paris. Although no direct link was ever made to question the safety of Concorde as a result of this crash, among the travelling public loyalty and patriotism played a large part in keeping faith with the Concorde dream. However, the Anglo-French design team would have needed no such anecdotal assurances; they new that Concorde was, as she proved over her entire life, a technological master-piece with a track record of safety and reliability to match any other passenger transport to date. Concorde would be caught out only by cruel and unforeseen twists of fate that have over the years bedevilled the best aeronautical engineering that man could devise.

By 1972 it was becoming clear to all those involved in the building of Concorde that the aircraft would quite

possibly never operate profitably. Both BOAC and Air France were getting cold feet and raising concerns about bringing Concorde into service. The British government gave assurances to BOAC that the public purse would offset any losses due to Concorde's financial inefficiency.

During 1973 Concord began to suffer a number of non-technical setbacks – politics and public demonstrations in North America, along with serious concerns regarding the economics of supersonic passenger travel, resulted in imposing damaging blows to Concorde's financial viability, with restrictions on schedule routes and cancelled orders. Pan Am, Quantas, TWA and Japan Airlines all withdrew their options to buy Concorde.

Adding to these problems, Concorde was not allowed to fly supersonic over Russia and India, ruling out schedules to the Far East.

It was a similar story in Africa where Nigeria refused to allow Concorde to refuel, preventing Concorde from

TIMELINE

1963
A total of 20 options are placed by the British Overseas Aircraft Corporation (BOAC), Air France and Pan American. The eight options placed by Pan American were cancelled.

1964
Fifteen more options are placed by BOAC, Air France, TWA, Continental Airlines, and American Airlines. Of these 15 options all but the four ordered by BOAC and Air France would be cancelled.

1965
Thirty-five options are placed for Concorde by Air Canada, Air India, American Airlines, Braniff,

Eastern Airlines, JAL Japan Airlines, Lufthansa, MEA, Quantas, Sabena, TWA and United Airlines. All these options were later cancelled.

1966
Four additional options are placed by Quantas, only to be cancelled later on.

1972-1984
Throughout these 12 years, despite interest from Iran Air and China, options and orders for Concorde ceased and the last remaining production aircraft were shared out between British Airways and Air France. In all, only 20 flying aircraft were ever built, of which seven went to Air France and seven to the British national carrier British Airways, formerly BOAC.

▲ *Sleek as a bullet, Concorde in a holding pattern over Southern England waiting for her clearance into Heathrow.*

flying regular scheduled flights to South Africa.

The news was no better in America. New York and Washington, D.C., had still not given the go ahead for Concorde to land. The only schedule available was Heathrow to Bahrain, and with limited passenger demand for this route only two to three flights each week were viable. The total order book now consisted of orders from Air France and BOAC only, but the Anglo-French partnership pressed on.

In hindsight it could easily be argued that the task of selling Concorde around the world was a doomed and almost impossible task. Aviation history is littered with bold and adventurous pioneering projects that cost their mentors fortunes as the huge white elephants collapsed. Often spurred on by a vision or a dream, aeronautical failures throughout the first half of the 20th Century are now well documented.

But times had changed and so had

the art of plane making. Airlines were now driven by passenger numbers, ticket pricing and the ever-elusive quest for profit in what hitherto had been a notoriously unprofitable industry. Whoever said 'the quickest way to turn a large fortune into a small fortune was to start an airline' was not far wrong. The world's airlines were beginning to understand well the needs of their ever growing market and had for years been dictating the specifications and operational requirements for new passenger airliners to the aircraft manufacturers.

▲ *Concorde pictured during a 'turnaround' at London Heathrow – re-stocking, re-fueling and maintenance checks are all carried out together.*

TIMELINE

February 1970
Well into its lengthy test programme, an Olympus 593 engine clocked up over 300 hours' non-stop operation on the test rig. This long run is the equivalent of 50 return transatlantic flights.

Palestinian leader Yasser Arafat seeks support from Soviets in Moscow.

March 1970
Now it is the turn of the British built prototype Concorde 002 to fly at Mach 1 for the first time.

More fighting in the Middle East as Israel clashes with Syria over Israel's occupation of Syrian Golan Heights. During the summer of 1970, civilians die in American race riots in Georgia, the Egyptian Aswan Dam is completed, the first of the major Notting Hill (London) race riots takes place, and British troops start using rubber bullets in Northern Ireland.

September 1970
Concorde 002 takes part in the Farnborough Air Show. Later that same month Concorde 002 lands at Heathrow airport creating what is probably the first round of public complaints regarding the noise created by Concorde's four mighty Olympus engines.

Palestinian terrorists hijack three passenger jets and land them in the desert in Jordan; the passengers are released and the planes are blown up. Also in September, Jimi Hendricks dies from a drugs overdose in London; the following month the same fate befalls Janice Joplin at the age of 27.

November 1970
A milestone month when both Concorde 001 and 002 achieve a major component of their design spec by reaching Mach 2.

President de Gaulle dies.

They also fully understood the cost of ownership and operating costs for each aircraft on a model by model and feature by feature basis.

So, despite the fact that Concorde, quite rightly, was driven into being by some of the passionate, visionary enthusiasm witnessed earlier in aviation history, from a commercial standpoint the project was severely flawed. Despite the fact that the British and French governments seemed to have created a manufacturing monster that was to ramp up the cost of developing and building Concorde, no one had ever properly completed the homework to estimate the true operating costs of Concorde in scheduled service. True enough, a full order book would have eventually balanced the development costs, but in order to fill the order book Concorde would have to be profitable in service. Perhaps too much weight was given to the image and prestige value that airlines would afford Concorde when staring down the barrel of the operating costs. Without government support, even the British and French flag carriers would probably not have ordered Concorde.

Somewhere in the back rooms of the Anglo-French consortium, in addition to turning a blind eye to the development costs, those involved were also avoiding the careful calculations of what it would cost the airlines to operate the airplane once in service. They had a correct gut feel that, but for the dogged support of the British and French governments, commercially, Concorde was another aviation white elephant.

THE JUMBO THREAT

In the early 1970s, following the most damaging oil shortage crisis in post-war history, fuel prices rocketed upwards at a time when the airlines were struggling to meet the ever increasing demands for cheaper air fares from the travelling public. The introduction of the Boeing 747 or 'Jumbo Jet' in 1969 possibly played one of the leading roles in Concorde's eventual demise. This huge new airliner satisfied the requirement for mass, cheap air travel while at the same time flooded the market with a glut of cheap empty seats on many of

▲ Final preparations for Concorde 002 at Filton before she is wheeled out to be presented to her public.

◄ 1969 – at last! Concorde 002 is finally unveiled to an admiring public at Filton

▲ In order to maintain the sleek body surface necessary for supersonic flight, Concorde is regularly cleaned and polished to a high sheen.

its early routes. Concorde was consigned exclusively to the very narrow high ticket price and curiosity market, and would never achieve the dream of supersonic air travel for the masses.

Only the British and French national airlines were able to take up the challenge of operating a supersonic passenger airliner, and even then only with huge government support. In truth, it is little wonder that the world's airlines did not embark on the supersonic adventure which was destined to drain airline profits in order to provide premium class travel to the privileged few. Thank heavens for aviation that British Airways and Air France were able to do so.

History will show that, in strict commercial terms, Concorde was not successful and the less generous would label her to have been a commercial failure. However, few if any 'commercial failures' have ever ruled the skies for 30 years as Concorde did. Only an aircraft with Concorde's pedigree could have survived the financial and political storms over those years. She was the first and is still the only supersonic passenger jet to enter scheduled service, carrying fare-paying passengers. Her engineering prowess is unquestionable and is witnessed by the fact that few would dare to deny that the retired Concorde fleet had 20 or more years of airline flying left in it. It is impossible to calculate the value of 30 years of

employing a highly sophisticated team of designers, manufacturers and operators of the aircraft. Last but not least, Concorde has excited, captured the imaginations and enhanced the life experience of millions of people spanning three generations. An aviation success, I think.

To say that Concorde's sales history was a roller coaster nightmare would be a dramatic understatement.

Constantly bombarded by political and financial prejudices and pressures, in addition to the technical and development mountains to climb, Concorde was offered no comfort by world events. However, Concorde did enter service and flew successfully with British Airways and Air France despite a catalogue of options, order placements, changes of mind and cancellations. ■

▲ Concorde on the airport concourse, pictured, by comparison, against a lumbering Boeing 747 'Jumbo Jet' which aptly demonstrates the contrasts between the two aircraft.

Chapter 5

Tupolev Tu-144 'Concordski'

▼ *The Russian-built Tupolev Tu-144 Supersonic Passenger Transport aircraft. For obvious reasons she was very quickly nicknamed 'Concordski'.*

It should be recognised that as well as all the many trials suffered by Concorde at the hands of politicians amid the fierce competitive world of aviation commerce, she was spared one other serious contender for her throne, the Russian-built Tupolev Tu-144.

There were other SST projects on the drawing board and some consumed billions of development dollars, but only two ever made it into the air. So it is that no account of Concorde would be complete without reference to a Supersonic Passenger Transport project that took to the skies some time ahead of Concorde. We may never know how close the Tu-144 may have come to challenging Concorde's unique aeronautical supremacy.

Looking at both aircraft, Concorde and the Tu-144 side by side, one could easily be forgiven for being convinced that one or other of the aircraft was copied from its counterpart. It was widely believed in Europe that the Russian secret service or KGB had stolen vital information and blatantly copied Concorde. However, although there is no doubt that espionage played its part in the development of the Tu-144, it was not a case of wilful and straightforward cheating. Alexei A. Tupolev, the famous son of a famous father Andrei, was unquestionably a talented and inspirational aircraft designer who was respected widely among aeronautical engineers

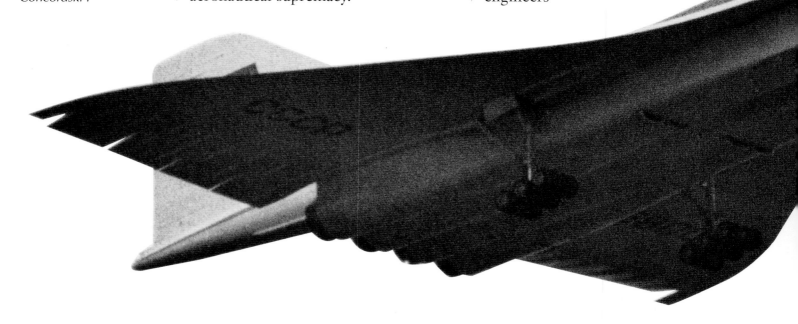

around the world, and he was probably copied a few times. Alexei Tupolev would not have needed and indeed would not have wanted to copy the Concorde or any other aircraft design, although he would have indulged in the normal scientific practice of learning from other scientists' published findings and experiences. He had proven over and over again that he was capable of the most innovative designs, being hampered only by the lack of modern computer-aided design and antiquated manufacturing techniques and facilities, not to mention real funding. When Tupolev first began to design his SST, the design criteria for Concorde had already been laid down many years before. Ideally Tupolev would have wanted to incorporate the latest aeronautical and engineering aeroplane, and these would have been somewhat more

advanced than when the Concorde design was conceived and finalised.

Yet again in the world of supersonic transport, political pressure was brought to bear, only this time it was the Russian political administration that exerted its influence. The Soviet leader Nikita Kruschev was determined to 'out-do' the West in as many areas as possible, across the full spectrum of world events from foreign policy, through technology, the arts and every conceivable situation that might gain global recognition on the world stage. Russia had been out-done and humiliated many times, but she was able to brush off the failures and pursue new successes with ease.

▼ The Tu-144 in landing configuration at the close of its maiden flight, escorted by a Russian military fighter plane.

In 1956 Russia came a narrowly contested second place in introducing the world's first jet passenger airliner when the prototype Tupolev Tu-104, the world's second jet passenger plane, landed at Heathrow airport for the first time. The project had been kept under wraps and stunned the world when newsreels recorded the arrival of Kruschev to Britain in the previously unannounced twin-engined passenger jet airliner. Having beaten the USA for second place in the passenger jet travel race he was now determined to beat the rest of the world in the race to carry passengers around the globe at supersonic speeds.

It is more likely that pressure from the Soviet government's ambitions rather than anything else that persuaded Tupolev to accept the large volume of Concorde secrets and include them in his own supersonic transport design. The KGB made many efforts to gain access to every aspect of the Anglo-French development plans and

drawings, both in Britain and in France. However, it was two key spies, one being a senior manager in the Russian airline Aeroflot in France, who were credited with gathering and passing on most of the stolen Concorde secrets.

Subsequently, in the late 1970s a third Russian spy was uncovered in France. The investigation into the third spy revealed that he had managed to obtain and send to Moscow a full set of blueprints for one of the French Concorde prototypes.

THE TUPOLEV CRASH

Officially, the cause of the Tu-144 'Concordski' crash at the Paris Air Show in 1973 has never been determined conclusively, so say the French and Russian air crash investigators and their respective governments.

Officially, the crash remains 'unexplained'.

In front of thousands of spectators at the show, and millions more around the world watching on television, the Russian airliner broke up in flight and

▲ *1956 – and Russia stuns the world when newsreels recorded the arrival of Nikita Kruschev to London's Heathrow Airport in the previously unannounced 'world's second' twin-engined, passenger jet airliner – the Tupolev Tu-104.*

TIMELINE

March 1971
By now the Americans fully realise that they are not going to achieve supersonic passenger travel with the current development programme. Washington withdraws its support for the American SST programme.

During the first three months of 1971 Idi Amin rose to power in Uganda, Rolls-Royce UK are declared bankrupt, decimal currency is launched in the UK, Apollo 14 lands on the Moon and civil war breaks out in Pakistan.

September 1971
Having been spotted near to completion at the back of the hangar at Filton when prototype 002 was first rolled out, now the first pre-production model Concorde 01 is officially rolled out at Filton.

During the summer months President Pompidou of France indicates that he is ready to see Britain join the EEC. In June the Soviets manage to dock a space capsule with the space station; later in the month three Russian cosmonauts are killed as the capsule returns to Earth.

December 1971
An important green light gets turned on in the USA when the Federal Aviation Agency concludes that Concorde meets American noise pollution control requirements.

Pre-production model 01 takes to the air for the first time and is delivered to the Concorde test base at Fairford in Gloucestershire.

War breaks out between India and Pakistan over Bangladesh; the USA steps up its bombing campaign over North Vietnam

fell from the sky onto the outer suburbs of Paris. Even though the commonly held view was that the Tu-144 was but a poor copy of Concorde, no one imagined that they would witness such a graphic and disastrous portrayal of those widely held views. After the crash, the myth grew: the Tu-144 was not well enough built... the materials used for construction were inferior to those used in Concorde... the Tu-144 could not cope with the stresses encountered while trying to mimic Concorde's breathtaking display earlier that same day... and so on.

None of this could be further from the truth. Tu-144 pilot Mikhail Kozlov was not trying to copy the Concorde display; he had arrived in Paris with the specific intention of outperforming Concorde from the start. The Russian aircraft that crashed that day was a brand new re-designed Tu-144 which had ironed out many earlier weaknesses and arrived in Paris straight off the production line at the Tupolev factory. Her design criteria and build had many innovative features that were considered superior to some of those in Concorde and may even have been adopted had the Anglo-French consortium had access to them.

The forward retractable canard wings placed just behind the cockpit gave greater control at low air speeds and actually generated about one fifth more extra lift for the supersonic airliner. New titanium alloys were used in the skin panels and, on paper, the Tu-144's performance specification was set out to surpass that of Concorde. She was designed to carry 140 passengers at Mach 2.4, as opposed to and surpassing Concorde's design criteria of only 128 passengers at Mach 2.0.

In truth and in hindsight, however, over time the Tu-144 did not live up to its ambitious design specification when pressed into service. Fundamental flaws that would not be uncommon in early versions of a brand new and complex airliner were never resolved in the final production models. The finished (or unfinished) product in service was sub-standard compared with Concorde, and the aircraft also suffered at least one more 'unexplainable' crash in the Soviet Union. But it was not only some of these design and subsequent line performance problems that caused the dreadful crash that fateful day in Paris.

NO TURNING BACK

The Russian pilots had planned a stun-ning display routine with the precise intention of out-flying Concorde. They had high hopes of attracting options and orders for new aircraft from the world's airlines that were gathered at the show. The Russians were also keen to seize any chance to 'out-do' the West whenever the opportunity arose, just as they had done on March 22, 1956, when sneaking aviation's second jet passenger transport – the Tupolev Tu-104 – onto the world stage by delivering the Russian president into Heathrow Airport for a state visit,

▲ June 1972 – Concorde 002, now registered as G-BSST, lifts off from the runway at Fairford at the start of its world sales tour. (See Timeline on page 80) The competition between the Anglo-French venture and the Russian Tu-144 was intense and rumours of espionage were rife.

TIMELINE

April 1972
After more than 20,000 hours of testing, the latest Olympus 593 Mk 602 engines are fitted to French pre-production Concorde 02 in Toulouse.

Apollo 16 lands on the Moon; earlier this year Britain formally joined the EEC; and the Queen Elizabeth ocean liner was completely destroyed by a fire as she lay at anchor in Hong Kong harbour.

May 1972
With three Concorde aircraft now flying, 001, 002 and 01, the total hours flown by Concorde pass the 1,000 mark.

The focus of attention is now on Concorde's order book. This month sees a major boost to sales when the British Overseas Aircraft Corporation (BOAC)

places options for five Concorde aircraft.

An Israeli airliner is hijacked and its 92 passengers are taken to Entebbe and held captive. Israeli special forces launch a bold and daring raid on the airport, freeing all of the hostages.

June 1972
From its test base at Fairford Concorde 002, now registered as G-BSST, lifts off the runway on its first leg of the marathon world sales tour. Flying to Australia via the Far East, Concorde would clock up more than 45,000 miles on this trip.

In the USA the Watergate scandal begins as bugging devices are discovered at the Democrat party headquarters. In the summer 11 Israeli athletes are killed by Arab terrorists at the Munich Olympics.

just four years after the Comet, the world's first jet passenger transport, went into service. That aircraft had been hugely successful, selling widely into the Communist bloc countries.

So why did we not see The Tu-144's scheduled display? One thing that does remain 'unexplained' is why the air show organisers, along with French air traffic control at Le Bourget airport, cut short the Tu-144's display time slot by 50 per cent. To make matters worse, the Russian crew were not advised of the reduced time available to them until they were sitting at the end of the runway preparing to take off and perform their planned routine. With so much at stake this would have put the two Russian pilots under enormous pressure. They would have had to quickly re-think their display schedule and prepare to put it straight into practice as they commenced their takeoff run.

Pilots of all display aircraft carefully plan and extensively practise their display routine well in advance of any show.

They programme attractive manoeuvres that they hope will impress those watching from the ground, and ensure that entry and exit from each manoeuvre complement the whole routine and provide optimum speed, height and position for each part of the display. The whole routine would be rigorously examined to ensure that the display was safe for both pilots and the watching crowds. No pilot wants to die looking good. Furthermore, crashing aircraft at public displays on the world stage does not fill order books.

All display flights – and indeed all aircraft flights – have a back-up plan in the event that something may go wrong, or in case a flight has to be cut short or diverted. But this was different – nothing had 'gone wrong' and there was no emergency that well qualified pilots would routinely respond to as a result of their high standard of training. By the time the Tu-144 was airborne, the crew would have been mentally extracting the most important manoeuvres

The Paris Air Show 1973. The Tu-144 has completed her programme and begins to follow the procedure for bringing the aircraft into land. Mistakenly she lined up on the wrong runway, and realising her mistake, and perhaps in an attempt to avoid embarrassment, applied full reheat and pulled up into a steep climb. It was this final manoeuvre that was to prove fatal.

ABOVE: *The Tu-144 after recovery from its near vertical roll, stalls and drops her nose into an almost vertical dive. It is clear that her pilot has lost control.*
ABOVE CENTRE: *To the horror of spectators on the ground the Tu-144 starts to break up in mid air before she hits the ground.*
FAR RIGHT: *The ill-fated airliner, now falling in pieces, rains down on to an unsuspecting residential suberb to the north of Paris. All the crew are killed.*

from their routine and patching them together in their minds in order to come up with a display now half the length in time of that originally planned. They would have been focused on the

handling of the aircraft so as to maintain safe entry and exit speeds, height and 'g' limits, while trying to give a smooth, impressive show.

The display appeared to proceed well, with only the better informed observers noting that it did not include all that they might have expected. To the uninformed, the display would have lived up to their preconceived notion that 'Concordski', as suspected, was not as good as Concorde.

Probably the first indication that there might have been pressure on the crew could have been noticed when, after completion of their display, they positioned incorrectly and began their final approach to the wrong runway for landing. This in itself was not particularly threatening; it happens from time to time and, along with other possible 'reasons for not landing', is quickly rectified by the crew carrying out a 'missed approach' (this used to be called 'going around'). The procedure involves applying full takeoff power, establishing a positive rate of climb, and then cleaning up the airframe by retracting the undercarriage then eventually flaps and other lift devices.

One would have expected air traffic control to pick up the error first and then inform the landing crew, along with giving instructions to re-position for a safe approach to the correct runway. In the case of the Tu-144, it would appear that it was the Russian crew who realised their own mistake and initiated the missed approach. Perhaps in order to disguise the error they applied full reheat and pulled up into an impressive steep climb. To the watching crowd and maybe even air traffic control this looked like a dramatic final stunt to end their display.

Although never acknowledged or admitted by the crash investigators, the Tu-144 was not the only aircraft occupying the skies over Le Bourget at that moment in time. The French military had been filming the Russian display from a camera mounted on a reconnaissance aircraft circling above the display area, or 'box'. As the Tu-144 climbed away steeply the Russian pilots would have seen a possible mid-air collision risk and would have taken avoiding action, in this case by pushing the nose sharply downwards to arrest the climb rate. This sudden and excessive change in the Tu-144's angle of attack (i.e. the angle of incidence between the airflow and the aircraft wing), triggered one or more devastating events.

This abrupt nosing-over manoeuvre would have almost certainly been outside of the aircraft's design envelope for flight. It possibly caused the wing to stall and lose lift, but certainly caused all four engines to 'flame out', leaving the stranded airliner with no power. The crew had only one chance left to correct the situation. Once again they pushed forward on the controls, just managing to harness enough remaining inertia in the aircraft's forward motion to cause the aircraft to nose over further into a dive. In what looked like a near vertical dive, the crew would have been watching the airspeed indicator that would have indicated the speed of the air which was rushing into the dead engine intakes. At an optimum point they would attempt to re-light the burners and, at a given airspeed, try to pull out of the dive.

We will never know how close they came to success. With just 1,500 to 2,000 feet between the Tu-144 and the ground, and with a windshield view consisting only of the ground, the crew attempted to pull up into a recovery from the dive. As the aircraft began to recover the wing loading in the port forward canard wing exceeded the design limits, and the wing detached. The airliner rolled slowly onto its back and began to break up into numerous pieces that rained down on to an unsuspecting residential neighbourhood in the north of Paris.

AFTERMATH

Despite the relatively limited extent of post-impact fire, mainly due to the wreckage falling in multiple smaller pieces over a large area, the two black box recorders carried on board were 'unexplainably' never found. Both the flight data recorder and the cockpit voice recorder were deemed to have been destroyed in the crash. This is a rare and unusual circumstance. Even in complete burn-outs of intact aircraft hulls, it is rare to lose one, let alone both, of the black box recorders, and it was even more unexpected given the odd circumstances surrounding this particular accident.

The investigation into the accident was carried out jointly by the Russian and French air accident investigation teams under the leadership of a French official. There is little doubt that the suggestion that a French military aircraft 'spying' on the Russian display had possibly contributed to the accident by causing the Russian crew to push the Tu-144 beyond its design limits. That would be too much to bear. Equally, the multiple engine failures and subsequent airframe failure of the Tu-144 seemed too much to admit in public. The real truth about the events that led up to and caused the accident were just too embarrassing for both the French and Russian governments.

As for the Anglo-French Concorde, her reputation was safe. In the absence of an official and true accident report, the admiring British and French public would assure themselves that the Soviets had fallen foul by stealing Concorde's design and producing an inferior and unsafe copy. No official report on the Tu-144 accident was ever published; it received the rubber stamp of 'causes unknown'. ∎

TIMELINE

December 1972
Costs for Concorde begin to soar as the British government nearly trebles its financial support for the production of Concorde; the cash injection for production aircraft now exceeds 350 million pounds.

American B-52 bombers still pounding Hanoi, the capital of North Vietnam. One month earlier the first American B-52 was shot down over North Vietnam.

January 1973
Having kick-started the American SST programme by placing controversial options for six Concorde aircraft 10 years before, Pan American Airlines (Pan Am) along with Trans World Airlines (TWA) cancel their Concorde options.

President Nixon finally stops the bombing of North Vietnam and a peace treaty is agreed.

March 1973
The Concorde order book begins to shrink as America's Continental Airlines cancels an option for three Concordes.

As the last of the US Army pulls out of Vietnam, in London 200 people are injured and one dies as a result of two IRA car bombs exploding on the streets.

June 1973
In front of thousands of spectators on the ground and the world's watching media, the Russian Tu-144 crashes onto a northern Paris suburb after displaying at the Paris Air Show. As well as the six crew on board the aircraft a further eight people are killed on the ground.

Chapter 6

Concorde in Service

The first departure of British Airways Concorde on a scheduled flight was to Bahrain on January 21, 1976. Almost simultaneously, an Air France Concorde departed Charles de Gaulle airport in Paris on her first scheduled flight to Rio de Janeiro, Brazil. By the time Concorde entered service she had cost nearly one billion pounds to develop, this being equally divided between Britain and France. However, by 1976 Concorde was all but fully developed and cancellation on economic grounds at this stage made no sense.

Following the cancellation of the failed American SST project in 1971,

and the cancellation of their respective Concorde options by Pan Am and TWA in 1973, US resistance to any

▼ *The cockpit flight crew of the first British Airways Concorde flight to Bahrain.*

other SST project and particular Concorde was widespread. This was presented on the grounds of noise and air pollution, plus a growing awareness of the need for conservation of the environment and the rate at which the world was using up its oil reserves.

OPPOSITION AND FEARS

There were unfounded scare stories regarding ozone layer damage, or even depletion, and the unknown effects and possible damage caused by the infamous sonic boom. The fears surrounding the sonic boom were resolved by operating routes where transition to supersonic flight would occur mainly over the oceans or scarcely populated areas. Furthermore, extensive research into the chemical changes in the upper atmosphere caused by Concorde showed that the aircraft would have a negligible effect on the ozone layer, certainly considering that the latest projections envisaged a total world-wide Concorde fleet of only 20 to 30 aircraft.

Extensive development of Concorde's air intakes and efflux management had gone as far as possible to mediate the

▼ *The first departure of a British Airways Concorde on a scheduled flight took off on January 21, 1976 from London, Heathrow to Bahrain.*

▲ *May 1976 marked the arrival of the British Airways Concorde just one minute after the arrival of the Air France Concorde. The two aircraft taxied ceremoniously around Dulles International airport and ended up parked nose to nose for a memorable photo-shoot.*

higher jet engine noise that would be inevitable during the takeoff and landing phases of Concorde's flight. With careful planning of arrival and departure routes, plus prudent management of the powerplants by pilots during descent and departures, would further help to reduce the noise levels on the ground. However, to refine these practices would take many years, and as Concorde went into service she was unquestionably noisier than her

operators would have liked, thus playing into the hands of the noise pollution lobbies particularly in the USA.

In practice, by the time that Concorde was flying scheduled services in and out of New York, the noise abatement measures were working well. And, because there were just four flights per day, the noise campaigners had little evidence to present to politicians or the general public. Resistance to Concorde on environmental grounds became a

By 1976, only the Iranian national carrier Iran Air and China Airlines remained as serious potential customers for Concorde. The pressure was on British Airways and Air France to fill the Concorde order book and justify the British and French governments' investment and support for the two Concorde production facilities in Filton and Toulouse.

The breakthrough came in February 1976 when the US Secretary for Transport gave the go ahead for two Concorde arrivals and departures per day in Washington, D.C., and four arrivals and departures each day in New York. These slots were to be shared equally between Air France and British Airways.

INTO THE USA

The first of these services to Washington were inaugurated during May of 1976 with the arrival of the British Airways Concorde just one minute after the arrival of the Air France Concorde. The two aircraft were taxied ceremoniously around Dulles International airport and were parked nose to nose for a photo-shoot before taking their passengers to the stands. However, the flights into New York were seriously delayed and were not inaugurated until October of 1977, with the full four services per day commencing one month later in November.

In December 1977 British Airways used their existing Bahrain route to provide an onward Concorde service to Singapore. Although all of the flight crews would be British Airways staff, the cabin services crews would be rotated between British Airways and Singapore Airlines staff. Originally, it had been intended to fly supersonic-

hobby-horse to a relative minority of mainly New Yorkers.

In fact, soon after the commencement of scheduled Concorde services to Bahrain, many voices in the USA were acknowledging that much of the American resistance to Concorde was based on jealousy over the fact that she was not American built. This was a view expressed by no lesser person than the director of design at the giant Boeing Corporation.

TIMELINE

June 1973
The dramatic Concorde specification is finally put to good use. Concorde 001 takes scientists from around the world to the edge of space (55,000 feet) to view the solar eclipse at nearly twice the speed of sound. At this speed, Concorde follows the footprint of the eclipse, allowing the scientists to observe it for over an hour.

There are now 27,000 British troops on the streets of Northern Ireland.

September 1973
The French pre-production Concorde 02, now registered as F-WTSA, arrives in America for the first time. Landing at newly opened Dallas – Fort Worth airport she is urgently seeking the support of the American people and their aviation legislators.

Author of 'Lord of The Rings', J. R. R. Tolkien, dies.

▲ The Concorde lounge
at London Heathrow
Airport.

▶ The main entrance to
the VIP Concorde lounge
at London Heathrow.

▲ The Concorde lounge at New York's JFK International Airport.

◄ The VIP Concorde lounge at New York's JFK International Airport.

through Indian airspace and some successful test flights had been completed earlier. However, by the time the service was due to commence, permission to overfly Indian territory at supersonic speeds had been withdrawn by the Indian government. This meant that Concorde was forced to take a more southerly route over the ocean. Although this added over 200 miles to the route, in Concorde this added only 10 more minutes of flight time. The

36 09

▲ This is British Airways Concorde – G-BOAD – leaving London Heathrow. She sports the standard British Airways livery on the hidden (starboard) side of the aircraft while flying the colours of Singapore Airlines on the visible (port) side.

aircraft's range and endurance were becoming significantly enhanced and perfectly practical.

Unfortunately, this route was quickly compromised once again, this time by the Malaysian government who withdrew permission for Concorde to fly supersonic over parts of its territory. Although this was finally resolved, with the resumption of the schedule in January 1979, it was to last only another 20 months before the service was finally withdrawn in November 1980.

In its time this particular service had set another first in Concorde's career: for the first time Concorde had flown with a livery other than that of British Airways or Air France. A single British Airways Concorde, G-BOAD, had primarily been used on the service and sported the standard British Airways livery on one side of the aircraft while

flying the colours of Singapore Airlines on the other side.

In June 1980, the only other scheduled Concorde service by a branded partner airline came to a close. In the USA, Braniff Airways had been operating a subsonic Concorde service between Washington and Dallas, Texas. Braniff had earlier ambitions to introduce long haul supersonic services within the Americas, but the tide was turning against them, as with all of the world's airlines. Deregulation of the American airlines brought ever more pressure, with cheaper airline seats flooding the American market. Dwindling passenger numbers and rising fuel costs eventually brought this Concorde venture to an end.

Following the cancellation of these services, in 1982 Air France brought to a close a range of Concorde services that had served South American

destinations and also their Paris to Washington route. British Airways would continue with their London to Washington schedule for another 12 years, finally withdrawing the service in October 1994. It had been possible to continue on to Miami from Washington by Concorde for some time but this extension of the Washington route was withdrawn by British Airways in 1991.

Despite the fact that the cessation of scheduled services is normally driven by a lack of profitability, there was a benefit component to these cancelled routes. Concorde, though still performing outstandingly, was by now an ageing aircraft type of which only 14 viable production aircraft had been built. The fleet was not big enough to support the multiplicity of scheduled services offered by other more prolific aircraft types. By releasing Concorde from

these cancelled routes, the solid and regular New York schedule, along with the rising number of profitable charter flights, benefited from better availability and serviceability within the British Airways Concorde fleet.

Following a 1979 British Airways

▲ TOP: *A simultaneous landing of Air France and British Airways Concordes at Miami International Airport.*
Above: After landing the aircraft taxi in procession to the terminal.

THE FIRST FEMALE CONCORDE PILOT

ABOVE: As a British Airways Captain, Barbra Harmer was the first woman to pilot a supersonic airliner – Concorde. RIGHT: Here she is shown in Concorde's cockpit being congratulated by Captain Jock Lowe.

▶ Two 20th Century icons that are no longer with us. As Concorde cruises over Manhattan Island, New York the twin towers of the World Trade Centre are clearly visible to the left of the picture.

review of Concorde operations, the British government decided to write off the debts for the British Airways acquisition costs for five Concorde aircraft and spares. Under the deal, British Airways would pay back to the government 80 per cent of the bottom line profits from Concorde operations.

Toward the end of the 1970s, the full realisation of Concorde's financial condition and fate was becoming fully clear to both the British and French governments and their respective national carriers. The rest of the world's airlines had also demonstrated their understanding of the situation in cancelling their options to purchase Concorde one by one. In 1977, Aérospatiale had dismantled and scrapped their Concorde production jigs. Then, in 1978, the British Concorde production jigs were dismantled and transferred to Wroughton airfield in Wiltshire, where they were stored.

For Britain alone, the cost of Concorde to date had now reached nearly one billion pounds, and there was more yet to pay. Costs for the support given by the manufacturers of Concorde to keep her flying would need to be met by government, along with the cost of keeping a non-flying full test bed for Concorde at the RAE Farnborough. Eventually, in 1980, it was formally announced that the Concorde production line was closed and that no more Concorde aircraft would be built. Accordingly, the British production jigs were removed from storage and sent to the scrap yards. The scrapping of the test rig at Farnborough would later prove to be a near-fatal blow to Concorde when she was being prepared for return to service following the yet to happen Paris crash of an Air France Concorde.

June 1996 saw the 50th anniversary of Heathrow Airport. To celebrate the occasion, an historic fly past of some of Britain's finest aircraft was organised. Aircraft representing passenger travel of the past and the current day joined

TIMELINE

September 1973
The records begin to tumble as Concorde 002 returns from Washington to Paris in a new record time of 3 hours and 33 minutes. This record would be broken many more times during the following years.

Juan Peron becomes President of Argentina

October 1973
Just four-and-a-half years after first taking to the air, French prototype Concorde 001 has fulfilled her role and, after nearly 400 flights and over 800 flying hours, she is gracefully retired to the French Air and Space Museum at Le Bourget airport.

Once again in the Middle East, Arab troops spearheaded by Egypt and Syria launch a damaging surprise attack on Israel. Israeli troops win the war on the ground and push back the invading forces, with the Israelis themselves now advancing into Syria and Egypt.

June 1974
New routes are now being tested and French pre-production model 02 covers the return journey from Paris to Rio de Janeiro in just under 13 hours.

Now desperate to win the hearts and minds of the Americans, Air France stages a mind-blowing demonstration of Concorde's unrivalled capabilities. In the morning of June 17 a French-built Concorde departs from Boston on route to Paris at exactly the same time as an Air France Boeing 747 departs Paris on route to Boston. Not only does Concorde cover four times the distance of the 747 by the time they pass each other, but she lands in Paris and after a one hour turn around, flies back to Boston, passing the 747 once again on the way, completing the round trip more than 10 minutes ahead of the 747's one way crossing.

At Wimbledon this year Americans Jimmy Connors and Chris Evert take both of the singles crowns. One month earlier 20,000 people are killed by an earthquake in the Chinese province of Sichuan.

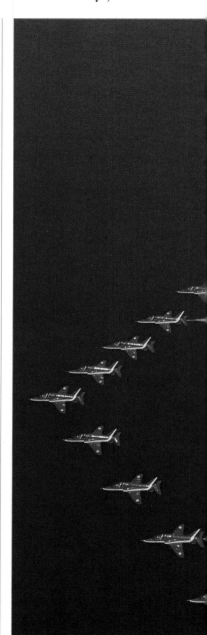

the Battle of Britain Memorial Flight to set a dramatic backdrop for the famous 'Concorde in formation' with the RAF Red Arrows aerobatic display team.

THE GLORY YEARS

By the mid-1990s, travelling transatlantic by Concorde was only £1,200 to £1,500 pounds more expensive than the £4,500 fare for albeit first class but subsonic carriage in a conventional passenger jet. This difference in ticket price for the rich and famous, along with those business travellers for whom time really was money, was really negligible, representing about a 20% premium for the convenience, privilege and prestige of flying Concorde.

These were becoming her glory years. She continued to break records and progressed to more than qualify for all of the aviation superlatives that were heaped upon her. She still astounded generations of passengers and Concorde worshipers, but now British Airways Concorde operations were both commercially desirable and profitable.

▶ OVERLEAF: Concorde G-BOAG in flight emphasises the sheer beauty of this outstanding 20th century aviation icon.

▼ Concorde escorted by the Royal Air Force aerobatic team, the 'Red Arrows', flies in formation above the QE2 to celebrate a new travel offer – passengers travel one way across the Atlantic in supersonic luxury and return in more leisurely stately grandeur.

FLYING THE FAMOUS

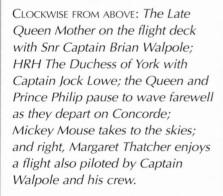

CLOCKWISE FROM ABOVE: *The Late Queen Mother on the flight deck with Snr Captain Brian Walpole; HRH The Duchess of York with Captain Jock Lowe; the Queen and Prince Philip pause to wave farewell as they depart on Concorde; Mickey Mouse takes to the skies; and right, Margaret Thatcher enjoys a flight also piloted by Captain Walpole and his crew.*

It was during this period in her illustrious career that Concorde joined forces with a former flagship of British transatlantic travel, the QE2 ocean-going liner. The emergence of viable passenger air travel across the Atlantic culminating in the ultimate supersonic service now provided by Concorde had long relegated mass passenger sea-going transatlantic crossings to the history books. But now, with growth of Concorde charters aimed at 'once in a lifetime' supersonic experiences, for the more regular traveller a new package was on offer. With the link-up of P&O shipping lines and British Airways one could travel one way across the Atlantic enjoying the ultimate in flying at Mach 2 at the edge of space, then return in the sedate but supreme luxury on the QE2. Along with a number of other regular Concorde charter companies, Concorde charter flights eventually accounted for more than 10 per cent of

*TOP ROW FAR LEFT:
A flambuoyantly uniformed
Spanish Guard watches
over Concorde on her first
flight to Barcelona.*

CENTRE LEFT: *Passengers
receiving the typically
friendly and sumptuous
on-board service.*

LEFT: *The three elements
necessary to get every
Concorde flight into the
air pose for the camera,
the Flight crew, the Cabin
crew and the Engineering
crew.*

BOTTOM ROW FAR LEFT:
*Elaine and Estelle Moffat,
identical twins serving
aboard Concorde and
who were soon dubbed
'The Supersonic Twins'*

CENTRE LEFT: *An engineer
carries out a routine
under-carriage check
between flights.*

LEFT: *A pipe band plays to
celebrate the roll out of
the new Landour livery in
1984.*

all supersonic passenger travel.

In 1996 the Concorde fleet potential was assessed for a life extension pro- gramme. The conclusion was that the Concorde fleet on average was only at the half-way stage of its flying career. Concorde had now been in service for 20 years and was good for another 15 years at least. These inspection results confirmed that Concorde could still be flying the regular scheduled London to New York service beyond the year 2020.

In hindsight, one can only assume that the final decision to ground Concorde in 2003 went way beyond operational or commercial considerations.

Throughout Concorde's later service life, a number of new or re-manufac- turing processes had to be carried out. Fortunately, or, perhaps more correctly, due the high standards of the original Concorde design and build quality, there were few relatively inexpensive modifications that needed to be

▲ 1984 – The first pictures of the new Landour livery pictured here at Prestwick Airport, Scotland which was regularly used for training Concorde staff.

implemented. Not including the modifications carried out following the Paris crash in 2000, at around £7million, perhaps the most expensive modification would have been the redesigned rudder sections. Even then, this modification was more expensive than it should have been because the original production jigs had been scrapped years earlier and new ones had to be built.

Over time, some of Concorde's flight avionics systems (originally designed to 1960s standards) were updated to more modern systems, as was normal practice for any aircraft extending active service through new technology development phases. Other than this short and mostly standard list of modifications, relatively

▲ First inflight pictures of the last livery that was to adorn Concorde. It was launched in 1998 and was known as the Chatham Livery.

◄ Concorde and a Boeing 747 pose nose-to-nose at London, Heathrow to show off their new look.

very little needed to be done in order to keep Concorde in service. This is an unquestionable testament to the fact that Concorde, born in the early 1960s, was still years ahead of her time as she continued supersonic services into the 21st Century. Sadly, the last Concorde to undergo the 12,000 hours check was Concorde 214, registered as G-BOAG. This involved stripping the aircraft back to bare metal and down to the basic airframe in order to carry out fatigue and corrosion checks. Following the untimely grounding of the Concorde fleet, no Concorde will now see a second 12,000 check.

Experience gained in Concorde operations, and indeed all intelligence

TIMELINE

October 1974

There are now six Concorde aircraft flying and the total of Concorde flying time passes 1,000 hours.

Throughout the summer numerous world leadership roles change hands. Juan Peron dies in Argentina, in Greek Cyprus the Greek Colonels and Archbishop Makarios are deposed, along with Emperor Haile Selassie in Ethiopia. In the USA Richard Nixon resigns over Watergate and is replaced by Gerald Ford. In October Muhammad Ali regains the world heavyweight boxing title. Before the year ends, 28 people are killed in IRA bomb attacks on the British mainland.

May 1975

The French authorities issue production aircraft Concorde 203, registered F-WTSC, with its provisional Certificate of Airworthiness.

During the opening months of 1975 Margaret Thatcher became leader of the Conservative party and a tube train crashed into the buffers at Moorgate station, London, killing 35 commuters. In Cambodia the Khmer Rouge captured Phnom Penh, and in neighbouring Vietnam, southern capital Saigon fell to North Vietnamese troops.

June 1975

Back at Fairford, the first British Airways pilots begin flying training on Concorde. Later this month the British Civil Aviation Authority grants British built production Concorde 204, now registered as G-BOAC after British Airways' former name, its own provisional Certificate of Airworthiness.

A referendum is held in the United Kingdom confirming that Britain remains within the EEC.

September 1975

Concorde 204 trials a new route from London to Newfoundland and sets a new record by making the transatlantic round trip twice in one day.

Israel and Egypt sign an accord on the Sinai Desert, brokered by world peace envoy Henry Kissinger.

October 1975

Concorde receives a full French Certificate of Airworthiness.

No let up in the fighting in Northern Ireland. The IRA has already been outlawed and this month the Ulster Volunteer Force is banned also.

▶ The shimmering heat of the engine afterburners combined with the sultry heat of the Caribbean is clearly seen as Concorde lifts off from Barbados for the return journey to London.

▼ The huge task of painting Concorde goes on in the paint shop at London Heathrow. Pictured here in 1998 Concorde is getting her new Chatham livery.

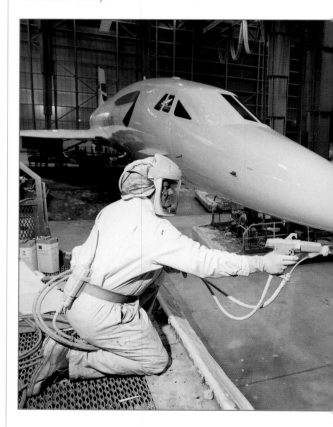

gathered through the world-wide operation of subsonic fleets, resulted in the upgrading of flight planning, air traffic control and other airline procedures that could be deployed in order to further enhance Concorde's route performance.

Today's air traveller is fully familiar with internet bookings and e-tickets, along with fast self-service automated

check-in facilities available at many large airports. These systems enable the traveller to cut down booking and check-in delays to a minimum. Few people other than Concorde passengers will recognise that these are modern electronic versions of existing sophisticated systems introduced in support of Concorde operations. Early on it was realised that crossing the Atlantic in three and a half hours was somewhat spoiled by having to spend two hours in the airport prior to departure. Telephone check-in, fast-track baggage and passenger processing through the airport, dedicated Concorde lounges – all have been enjoyed by Concorde passengers for many years. ▪

Chapter 7

The Paris Crash

Although there are reportedly undocumented accidents in Russia involving Tu-144 aircraft on internal mail flights, ironically and tragically, the only two documented air crashes in history involving supersonic passenger airliners both happened in Paris, killing the crews, passengers and

innocent victims on the ground. The first was the Russian Tu-144 prototype in 1973 (see Chapter 5). The second, the lowest point in Concorde's history, occurred on July 25, 2000. Air France Concorde flight number AF4590 took off from Charles De Gaulle airport, Paris and crashed down on to a hotel in the district of Gonesse just 90 seconds after takeoff. This was just one mile from Paris and also just a mile short of a potential safe landing site for AF4590 at Paris Le Bourget airport. Had AF4590 managed to maintain sufficient power for a matter of just a few seconds' worth of extra flying time,

she may well have stood a chance of making a forced landing at Le Bourget, potentially saving many, if not all, of the lives on board.

FIRE BENEATH THE WING

The aircraft had caught fire under the left wing during its takeoff run. The damage caused the left undercarriage to jam in the down position and was compromising the power available from the left side engines. It is generally accepted that the primary cause of the accident was a tyre burst on the left-hand undercarriage caused by metal debris left on the runway by another

▲ An amateur snapshot captures the dramatic last moments of flight number AF4590 as she struggles into the air from Charles de Gaulle airport.

◄ ... and just 90 seconds later – the dreadful scene of devastation on the ground where the stricken aircraft crashed on to a hotel in nearby Gonesse.

▲ The burning remains of the hotel at Gonesse. When flight AF4590 came down she was just one mile from a potential safe landing at Le Bourget airport.

▶ The fire had prevented the left-hand undercarriage from being retracted. This compromised the power available to the aircraft and prevented her making the airfield at Le Bourget. Lying in the wreckage, right, is an almost complete undercarriage leg unit.

aircraft. The damaged tyre threw up more debris which ruptured the Concorde fuel tanks.

However, some speculation has suggested that a spacer not refitted to the undercarriage during recent maintenance had also caused a mis-alignment of the main undercarriage wheels after the tyre burst. The damaged undercarriage caused the

airliner to veer to the left, taking out a runway light at the edge of the runway. In order to avoid running out of control onto the grass, the pilot would have been forced to rotate (takeoff) early in the takeoff run, with a tail wind and at a speed lower than the optimum required for a clean takeoff and efficient climb out. The jammed undercarriage caused massive drag; power available to the pilot was reducing, and the aircraft was possibly unable to reach a safe climbing speed.

At 4.44pm, 90 seconds after leaving the runway at Charles de Gaulle, and possibly just 20 seconds short of the threshold at Le Bourget, Concorde AF4590 stopped flying and crashed to the ground, killing all of the crew, 100 tourists, mostly German, and four of the staff at the hotel on which the wreckage landed.

How could this happen? Why now, after 30 years in service? Why, indeed?

AN ACCIDENT WAITING TO HAPPEN?

Concorde had experienced 57 previous incidents involving burst tyres on take

▲ *Concorde had been subject to a number of burst tyre incidents prior to Paris which was a natural concern for the engineers. Here they are seen examining the under-carriage retraction system.*

TIMELINE

December 1975
Concorde receives a full British Certificate of Airworthiness.

After months of much televised public hearings in the USA, the American government delivers a crushing blow to Concorde's hopes of commercial success. Concorde is banned from landing anywhere in the United States of America for six months.

Air France takes delivery of its first production Concorde, number 205, which is registered as F-BVFA. Later in this month, just two years after the tragic accident in Paris, the Tu-144 enters service in the Soviet Union, carrying mail and freight between Moscow and neighbouring Kazakhstan.

The end of 1975 saw the close of two long-running regimes. In Angola the Portuguese gave up Angola after more than 300 years of colonialism, and in Spain General Franco died after 36 years as Head of State.

January 1976
British Airways takes delivery of its first production Concorde, British-built Concorde 206, now registered as G-BOAA. Also this month, British Airways and Air France commence scheduled Concorde services, British Airways flying between London and Bahrain and Air France flying from Paris to Rio de Janeiro via Dakar.

Two world-renowned artists die this month: British author Agatha Christie and American singing actor Paul Robeson.

February 1976
Just two months into Concorde's six-month American ban, the Head of Transportation in the US government reverses the ban and both British and French airlines are cleared to run limited daily Concorde scheduled services into New York and Washington for a 16-month trial period.

Millionaire heiress Patty Hearst stands trial for her part in a bank robbery.

May 1976
British Airways and Air France Concordes land simultaneously at Washington's Dulles airport marking the start of scheduled Concorde services on the route.

2,000 people are killed in an earthquake in Italy.

off; 13 of those incidents had resulted in damage to engines and six had resulted in the rupturing of fuel tanks. On June 14, 1979, Air France

Concorde flight 054 took off from Washington Dulles airport in the USA. Just before rotation the flight crew heard and felt two dull thuds from the rear of the aircraft. The crew were then informed by air traffic control from the tower that they could see what appeared to be flames in the vicinity of the port (left) engine bay. Less than two minutes into the flight a stewardess reported to the captain that a passenger had observed debris flying past the window during takeoff.

Now airborne, the crew could not retract the aircraft's main undercarriage and, amid an array of flight deck warning alarms, they flew past the control tower to gain a visual report of the aircraft's condition. Air traffic controllers confirmed that two tyres on the port undercarriage had deflated and broken up during takeoff. They then decided to divert to New York's

JFK airport. Within 15 minutes, hydraulic systems on the aircraft were failing and the crew put out a May Day, deciding to return to Washington Dulles in order to take advantage of the longer and wider runways there.

Ten minutes later and 25 minutes into the flight, the aircraft landed back at Dulles airport, grossly overweight despite having dumped fuel on the return leg, and using up nearly all of the 10,500 feet of usable runway. American and French air accident investigators later reported that the aircraft fuel tanks were breached in numerous places, fuel was leaking badly, and damaged wiring in the landing gear bay had caused a fire and prevented retraction of the undercarriage.

Given that Air France flight 054 was able to climb away, maintain altitude for 25 minutes and carry out a safe controlled landing despite having ruptured and leaking fuel tanks, an in-flight fire and a stranded main undercarriage, one can only conclude that on July 25, 2000, it was the barely reported additional factors that possibly turned flight AF4590's emergency into a fatal air accident.

GROUNDED

Immediately after the Paris crash the French aviation authorities ordered the grounding of Air France's Concorde fleet, but amid much controversy, British Airways continued with their Concorde flight schedule. The press speculated on many theories, including terrorism, bird strikes and cracks in the wings. Then on August 15, 2000, in response to the publication of a preliminary crash report, the Civil Aviation Authority in the UK withdrew Concorde's Certificate of Airworthiness, so grounding the BA fleet.

▲ ABOVE: *Concorde had previously suffered from tyre burst incidents on take-off. After the Paris crash she was fitted with new more resilient tyres.*

ABOVE LEFT: *Once Air France and British Airways had grounded their entire fleets, every aspect of Concorde's mechanical, electronic and hydraulic systems were checked thoughout. There was no stone left unturned in the effort to isolate the causes of the crash.*

TIMELINE

November 1976
With production aircraft now flying scheduled services, the Concorde flight test team at Fairford pack their bags and their equipment and return to Concorde's production base at Filton near Bristol.

Jimmy Carter is elected as the 39th President of the United States of America.

January 1977
Concorde has now been in service for just over a year has flown 3,500,000 miles carrying more than 45,000 fare-paying passengers.

Former British Prime Minister Anthony Eden dies, and the IRA are still bombing London.

May 1977
In May 1927, Charles Lindburgh flew the single engined 'Spirit of St. Louis' from New York to Paris in 33 hours and 29 minutes. Fifty years later Concorde retraces Lindburgh's steps, beating his record by 29 hours and 45 minutes.

Later this summer, in August, one great aeronautical achievement is followed by two great losses. The space shuttle flies for the first time and both Elvis Presley and Groucho Marx die.

November 1977
Royalty gets in on the act by choosing to fly Concorde on their return flight from Barbados.

After getting the go ahead it takes just three months to inaugurate scheduled Concorde services between Europe and Washington. The New York route had been a tougher nut to crack with far more opposition from noise abatement lobbies. Only now could British Airways and Air France commence scheduled Concorde services into New York.

During a year of brokering peace both with Israel and Libya, President Anwar Sadat of Egypt visits Israel and addresses the Israeli parliament.

Never before in aviation history had a single aircraft type been grounded following a single accident. Many people voiced the opinion that moves to ground Concorde were exacerbated by political interference and the desire by some bodies to bring the operation of Concorde to an early end, irrespective of the Paris crash or its causes.

After the July 25 crash, the French Air Transport Minister, clearly not wishing to risk a possible subsequent accident, wasted no time in grounding the Air France fleet. At the time of the accident, Air France Concorde F-BVFC had recently arrived in New York from Paris. She was now stranded and remained so for more than six weeks until the French Aviation Ministry obtained support from the USA, Britain and Ireland to allow the aircraft to return to Paris on a temporary Airworthiness Certificate. This was granted with a number of restrictions, including the fact that no passengers of any kind would be allowed on the flight. Such was the concern that on her return to Paris Concorde was greeted by the airport's fire services on full alert.

Early hopes, particularly in the UK, had been that the focus of the enquiry results would point to better codes of practice by airport authorities regarding keeping the runways free of debris and that only small changes to aircraft operating procedures would be required. A great deal of emphasis had been put on the different undercarriage features between the Air France Concorde and the British Airways Concorde fleets. British Airways had fitted different arrangements for water deflection and used different tyres to those of the French aircraft. The implication was that a British Airways Concorde would not have sustained the same damage in similar circumstances and therefore would not have crashed. These ideas were ruled out by British Airways, Air France and Aérospatiale, who all realised that the solution was not that simple and that keeping a united front and approach would best protect all of their respective interests

Even so, unlike the French, British Airways did not expect their Concorde fleet to be on the ground for long and pressed ahead with their operation plan, including another refit of the cabin interior. However, by September all parties were beginning to realise that it was going to take a great deal of change and convincing arguments before the French and British aviation authorities would revalidate the Certificates of Airworthiness.

Eventually, the aircraft in each Concorde fleet were kept together at their respective home bases – Heathrow and Charles de Gaulle airports. The

▲ Depending on the nature of the service or repair work required, planes were often reversed in to the hangars, particularly if engines had to be removed or replaced.

British remained optimistic regarding the time that it would take to get Concorde back in the air. They set about the task of running continuous checks on the parked aircraft to ensure that their was no deterioration in aircraft engines and systems brought about by standing around on the ground. All aircraft really do like to be in the air and, rather like a car, will develop leaks, corrosion and stiffness if not in use.

Almost immediately following the accident, a combined working group was proposed and brought into being with the remit to move quickly towards regaining airworthiness certificates for Concorde. Manufacturers, airlines and governments from both Britain and France would pull together in a joint exercise to get Concorde safely back into the air.

The process got off to a good start, with the group holding its first meetings in September 2000 following the release of the preliminary accident report. However, in France, an air accident investigation has to work under the auspices of the local magistrate in whose district the accident has occurred. With no expertise in aircraft accident investigations, this arrangement conspired to hinder the accident investigators, to the particular frustration of non-French personnel.

British Airways and Air France well understood that they needed to get their Concorde fleets back into the air quickly, and that waiting for the definitive report from the accident investigation team was not an option.

WHAT WENT WRONG?

In conjunction with the manufacturers they pre-empted the conclusions of the final report and pressed ahead to design

a series of modifications that would eventually meet the requirements of both the British and the French aviation authorities. Even this process quickly began to get bogged down, with too many opinions chasing too little information. A small team of people, including BA chief Concorde pilot Mike Bannister and four representatives from Air France and Aérospatiale, got together under the guidance of Jim O'Sullivan, BA's technical and quality director, and came up with a plan. The key events that caused the tragedy, and which system failures contributed to those events, were identified as:

- Fuel leaking from the tanks and igniting in the undercarriage bay.

- The performance of the Olympus engines during the short flight that eventually led to the crash. The flight data recorders recovered from the crashed aircraft had logged 'engine surges' starting shortly after takeoff on its final flight.

- Failure of the undercarriage to retract after takeoff.

While the cause of the fire was fairly clear cut, engine performance and drag induced by the stranded undercarriage played a key role in preventing the stricken airliner from making it to Le Bourget, where she may have been able to carry out a crash landing that could possibly have saved lives.

When the second accident report was released, unexpectedly it revealed that the debris from the burst tyre had not penetrated the fuel tank from the outside but, in striking the tank, had caused a hydraulic shock wave within the fuel in the tank that had burst it from the inside. This, however, did not affect the planned modifications. The new modifications included the fitting

▲ *As soon as Concorde's servicing and safety checks are completed she is passed back from engineering and back into flight operations.*

of rubber (Kevlar) linings to the insides of the fuel tanks in order to automatically plug holes in the tanks should they become damaged; the lining would be forced into the holes by the pressure of the escaping fuel. The new Kevlar lining would also inhibit such a shock wave and would still prevent fuel from leaking from the tank however it was breached.

The modifications were fitted at a cost of one and a half million pounds per aircraft; this large sum of money was insignificant compared with the financial losses and image damage that British Airways would incur should Concorde fail to return to service. In bullish mode, British Airways rolled out the entire Concorde fleet for a photo-shoot; it was the first time that all seven aircraft had been photographed together.

The plan to implement the modifications was put into action. Two aircraft would be used in the project, British Airways Concorde G-BOAF was selected to be the prototype for all of the modifications. In support of the programme, Air France Concorde F-BVFB would be relocated to a military air base in the South of France, where she would carry out high speed taxi trials to test some of the modifications that would be fitted to the British Airways Concorde, Alpha Foxtrot.

These tests would investigate the effects that leaking fluids and hot gases would have on the performance of the Olympus engines. These effects had been fully studied using computer simulation, but the new trials would demonstrate and validate those results. It had been planned to fit Kevlar linings in the bottom of all of Concorde's fuel tanks, but weight considerations and maybe cost favoured selective fitting of the linings. The high speed tests would help identify which tanks needed to be protected and which did not.

In the end, six of Concorde's fuel tanks were lined, with 124 separate liners being installed in tanks five and eight alone. The Kevlar liners were around five feet by one foot and were bolted to the ribs within the tanks, allowing a small gap between the liner and the skin of the wing. Having fuel physically in contact with the outer skin of the wing played a key role in keeping the Concorde outer skin cool during supersonic flight.

Back in the hangars, engineers would replicate the hydraulic shock waves and the subsequent failure of the fuel tanks. Rolls-Royce would take the engine fuel and hot gas ingestion testing one step further and actually test an Olympus engine to destruction in order to

◀ OPPOSITE: *After the suspension of Concorde operations following the Paris crash the British Airways fleet was mothballed at Heathrow. This allowed them the first opportunity to photograph the whole fleet together.it was the first time that all seven aircraft had been together.*

▼ *Some of the extensive rigging installed at the British Airways engineering base at London, Heathrow allowing the engineers to reach every part of the aircraft.*

▲ *The giant Airbus A380, Aérospatiale's successful development, gave a boost to Concorde's recovery. She was fitted with virtually indestructible new tyres.*

determine the absolute limits to which the engine could tolerate the ingestion of fuel and hot gases.

The work programme was carried out by two shifts of 20 engineers covering 16 hours per day. Even with this resource at work it would take two and a half months to modify Alpha Foxtrot. It was anticipated that lessons learned during this first refit would rapidly reduce the time taken to modify the rest of the fleet.

Because key engineers were now working full time on Alpha Foxtrot, more technical engineering aspects of the interior facelift could not be carried out. However, British Airways could at least fit the planned new seating and went ahead with the first stages of the cabin refurbishment. Apart from this activity boosting image and morale, the new seats were designed to be much lighter than their predecessors and this weight advantage would help to offset weight gains caused by fitting the Kevlar fuel tank liners.

As the year 2000 came to a close, the first of the Kevlar liners were being fitted to Alpha Foxtrot, and by now British Airways were seriously thinking about dates for recommencing services, with the early summer of 2001 clearly in their minds.

Ironically, early in 2001 it was good news from another Aérospatiale development project, the giant Airbus A380, that gave a boost to Concorde's recovery programme. Tyre manufacturer Michelin was about to finish the development work on a brand new class of aircraft tyre for the A380. This new tyre was almost impossible to burst

and would remain intact if deflated.

Given that it is nearly impossible to create a flexible rubber pneumatic tyre that cannot be punctured, however, it is how the tyre behaves after being punctured and during deflation that matters. The existing tyres on Concorde had two major problems. First, they had a tendency to break up and be thrown around, including upwards during takeoff run failures. This was the recognised cause of the catastrophic damage to the underside off the wings and fuel tanks of the Air France Concorde in Paris. Second, they were not terribly strong; with one tyre out, the adjacent tyres sharing the now increased loading would be more prone to failure, creating a degenerating failure sequence. Concorde's new tyres would have to be twice as strong in the first instance, and be able to remain intact and functional, allowing the undercarriage to run true in the event of a tyre failure.

TYRES AND TESTING

In 2001 Michelin's new design came to the rescue. During tests, these revolutionary new tyres were able to continue functioning safely during multiple simulated takeoff and landing cycles, after having been deliberately punctured.

Concorde had now overcome the primary modification requirement. However, a second important modification, though simpler to develop and fit, raised a third major obstacle that was to call on the dedication and courage of a Concorde flight crew.

It had been decided that the fuel

▲ Michelin's new tyres, as used on the Airbus, did not break up when they punctured like Concorde's. Here the new design tyres are being fitted to a Concorde at Heathrow.

▲ ABOVE AND RIGHT: *Fitting each of the fuel tanks with individually formed Kevlar linings.*

tanks would be lined with individually formed Kevlar linings. In the event of damage to the external fabric of the fuel tank, these Kevlar panels would absorb shock waves through the tanks and temporarily seal fuel leaks through breaches in the outer skin, thereby maintaining integrity of the fuel tanks during the critical recovery period following damage on a takeoff run. This modification alone would probably have saved the passengers, the crew and those people on the ground lost in the Paris crash. The design fabrication and fitting of the linings would be awkward but relatively straightforward. Although the linings would add some weight to the airframe and slightly reduce the maximum fuel capacity of the tanks, some weight advantage had been gained with the introduction of the new Michelin tyres, which were lighter than their predecessors.

By running Concorde on the ground within a critical speed range from 130 knots to 180 knots, engineers could replicate airflow over the airframe that would have been present at the time of the initial fuel leak. The crews devised a procedure for raising the nose during high speed parts of the runs to replicate the angle of attack of the aircraft on the day of the accident. In order to utilise the full length of the runway and to ensure that the test aircraft stayed within the speed range for as long as possible, standard engine thrust was used without the extra boost of re-heat. By releasing water containing coloured dyes from points under the wing, including the point at which they believe that the fuel leak occurred,

readiness to accept a test engine from British Airways stores at Heathrow. The engine would need to perform within accepted tolerances when subjected to fuel leak and hot gas ingestion into the engine air intake.

Results of the tests showed that the engine could easily cope with fuel ingestion rates that might occur from leaks in the modified Concorde Kevlar-lined fuel tanks.

At the BAe factory in Warton, engineers built a reconstruction of the undercarriage and undercarriage bay, along with sufficient wing section, to represent the area of damage to the accident aircraft. Using a temporary wind source to represent airflow around the airframe during the takeoff run, the team was able to release fuel from the point of rupture and attempt to determine the most likely source of ignition.

Three potential sources of the spark were identified: an engine surge in the Olympus power unit, a spark from the electrical cables controlling the landing gear, or the engine reheat itself. It was found that a surge in the number two engine did indeed ignite escaping fuel under test conditions. However, this theory was ruled out because when engine surges recorded by the black box flight data recorder on board the crashed aircraft were correlated with video evidence of the outbreak of fire, the results showed that the surges occurred after the fuel was ignited.

To test the reheat theory, fuel was allowed to leak from the position where the fuel tank was breached and flow the full length of the engine bay into the area surrounding the after-burners. Once again the fuel was ignited. However, given the strength of the air

engineers could observe whether or not such leaks would find their way into the intakes of the engines. By the end of January the results of these tests did indeed show that Concorde's port engines would have been ingesting leaking fuel almost immediately after the fuel tank was ruptured. British Aerospace (BAe) and Rolls-Royce would now have to determine the effect that this unspent fuel ingestion into the Olympus air intake would have had on engine performance.

Back in the UK, by chance the original Olympus engine test bed had survived the scrapyard and was refurbished in

TIMELINE

January 1978
It is now two years since Concorde entered service and she has now carried in excess of 129,000 fare-paying passengers.

A General by the name of Pinochet is rising to ever increasing power in Chile. During the coming months Italian Prime Minister Aldo Moro is kidnapped and killed by the Red Brigade, and in Iran, opposition to the Shah erupts into bloodshed as the Ayatollah Khomeini patiently waits in Paris planning his triumphant return to Tehran.

August 1978
British Airways alone passes the 100,000 fare-paying Concorde passengers milestone.

During this year the world's Roman Catholic faith will have three different popes. In August Pope Paul VI dies; his successor Pope John Paul I survives only 33 days; by October the cardinals in Rome are choosing a third pope in a single year.

January 1979
Concorde has now been in service for three years and has flown nearly 22,000 flying hours, carrying 300,000 fare-paying passengers.

A fresh glimmer of hope for Concorde flickers in the USA. American airline Braniff leases no fewer than 10 Concorde aircraft from British Airways and Air France to commence a new subsonic Concorde service between Washington and Dallas-Fort Worth.

Finally the Shah of Iran makes his escape and seeks refuge in Egypt.

February 1979
Once again Britain's Royal family fly Concorde as the queen and Prince Philip fly out to Kuwait to commence a royal tour of the Middle East.

After spending 16 years in exile, the Ayatollah Khomeini returns to Iran and quickly sets up a new interim government.

flow over the airframe close to takeoff speed, the fire was mainly confined to the rear of the wing achieving limited forward progression under the wing.

To simulate the potential for electrical ignition, an ignition source was placed at the point where it is believed that electrical cables may have been damaged by tyre debris. Upon operation of the ignitor, a fire broke out, immediately engulfing the undercarriage bay and surrounding area. It could clearly be observed that this fire closely resembled the video footage of the burning aircraft, taken on the day of the accident.

Engineers could never be absolutely certain, but it seemed highly likely that the ignition source was electrical cables in the undercarriage bay which were damaged by debris from the break-up of the tyre. Part of the modification programme subsequently included extra physical protection for cabling in the undercarriage bay.

Originally, British Airways had estimated that it would take a month and a half to fit the new Kevlar liners to G-BOAF. Unfortunately, this process was thwarted by an unusual circumstance regarding the manufacture of production Concorde aircraft. Concorde was not produced on a mass-production scale and each production aircraft included small modifications during production that meant that no two aircraft were exactly the same. The Kevlar linings were manufactured from the original Concorde drawings, but when engineers came to fit them into Alpha Foxtrot's fuel tanks, they found that the spaces between certain components were slightly different from those shown in the drawings and the linings had to be modified or remanufactured.

As if that was not frustrating enough, engineers found that the holes through the linings, which were designed to allow fuel to flow through and be in contact with the wing skin for airframe cooling, were too big. This was not acceptable, since it compromised the lining's ability to sufficiently restrict the flow rate of escaping fuel in the

event of a fuel tank rupture. Once again the linings had to be modified, by filling all of the holes and re-drilling them to the correct size. There was, however, some compensation in that the latest test results now showed that only about a half of the planned 124 liners would need to be fitted and affected only six fuel tanks around the main undercarriage bays. Furthermore,

this of course was the first aircraft to be modified and lessons learned on this aircraft would dramatically reduce the time required for subsequent refits.

More good news came with the announcement that the new Michelin NZG tyres were getting through the test programmes with flying colours and would almost certainly be certified for use on Concorde. However, such is the

▲ *In anticipation of a return to service extensive servicing was carried out on the massive Rolls Royce engines.*

rigorous nature of aircraft certification, that when Air France F-BTSD, complete with new D check certificate, flew to a military air base for high speed taxi trials for the new tyres, she had to be fitted with the original Goodyear tyres for the trips to and from the air base – rather ironic as the Goodyear tyres, now known to be flawed, were certificated for use on Concorde, whereas their replacement Michelins were not.

By the end of May F-BTSD, complete with a new coat of paint, returned to Charles de Gaulle airport with a full set of Michelin NZG tyres fitted to the main undercarriage, while retaining the

original Goodyears for the nose wheels. Eventually, British Airways would also fit the Michelins to the main undercarriage while retaining original Dunlop tyres for the nose gear. One month later it was confirmed that the new tyre fit would be submitted for certification, along with the other modifications that had been carried out in order to regain Concorde's Airworthiness Certificate. At the same time, at Heathrow, British Airways were preparing G-BOAF for her taxi trials and subsequent air tests.

Concorde, having not flown for nearly a year, and having undergone the disturbance of certain areas and systems

◀ OPPOSITE: *Concorde taxis toward the runway for her very last flight to Barbados.*

◀ *For the very last time Concorde is seen against a beautiful Caribbean sky.*

TIMELINE

June 1980
Due to a lack of fare-paying passengers and increasing fuel prices, Braniff shut down their Washington/Dallas Concorde service.

During the first half of 1980 Robert Mugabe became prime minister of Zimbabwe; independence from Britain follows soon after. A huge volcanic eruption in the USA is caught on film as one fifth of Mount St. Helens is destroyed. Also televised is the end of the Iranian Embassy siege in London. 26 hostages are rescued; five terrorists shot dead and one captured. In the summer Henry Miller dies, and Bjorn Borg wins his 5th title in a row at Wimbledon . As the year ends, terrorism continues in Italy and France, and Ronald Regan is elected president of the United States. In December, the film world was already mourning the death of Peter Sellers aged just 54, when on December 8 John Lennon is murdered in New York.

that had not previously been touched, all of her systems had to be fully checked out before she could even taxi under her own power, let alone get airborne again. Furthermore, during G-BOAF's verification flights, she would carry test monitoring equipment in the rear of the passenger cabin, and this would remain in place during the first 50 passenger flights following her return to service.

Concorde's in-flight fuel management systems were complex. The fuel system had to deliver fuel to the engines during a wide variety of flight profiles, including during very high angles of attack (very 'nose up'). Also, during the flight, fuel would need to be transferred between forward and rear fuel tanks

distributed around the aircraft in order to maintain correct weight and balance and trim stability, again during a wide variety of in flight conditions. All of this meant that the fuel system had to be able to pump and move fuel around the system to a higher standard of efficiency and reliability than that required for most conventional airliners. The calculations showed that the fuel system would continue to work efficiently and safely, so all that was needed was some rigorous ground testing before Concorde could take to the air once more.

TESTING AND TENSION

There was one peculiar problem that no-one had forseen, Before Concorde

British Airways' Chief Concorde pilot Mike Bannister took control for the first test flight of the newly modified Concorde G-BOAF.

ABOVE LEFT: *The newly modified Concorde takes off from Heathrow for her extensive flight tests.*

first flew in 1969, a full-scale test rig of the fuel tanks and fuel systems was constructed at Farnborough. Simulated acceleration, deceleration and unusual nose-up, nose-down and turning manoeuvres were tested for all phases of Concorde's design flight envelope. It was not anticipated that any major design modifications to the fuel systems would be required in the future, and consequently, the test rig had long ago been broken up for scrap. Therefore, the new modifications could not be tested on the ground.

In July 2001, two senior Concorde captains, CAA test pilot Jock Reid and chief BA Concorde captain Mike Bannister, taxied G-BOAF, the first Concorde to receive the new modifications, out onto the runway threshold at London's Heathrow airport. They had both done this many times before and were obvious choices to carry out the forthcoming test flight. However, they were the first for many years to take a civil airliner carrying as yet untested and unproven modifications into the air for an 'air test'. Thankfully, the air test was a complete success. The return flight across the Atlantic proved that the computer modelling prior to the flight had been correct and, with a few 'tweaks' to the Kevlar linings in the tanks, Concorde was once again safe to carry passengers beyond the speed of sound.

Technically, neither British Airways nor any other airline could test fly G-BOAF since she did not have a current Certificate of Airworthiness. Under normal circumstances the temporary permit to fly should be issued to the manufacturer and be conducted by their own pilots. However, Airbus Industries, who were now Concorde's formal 'manufacturer' having absorbed Aérospatiale when Airbus was formed, did not have any Concorde pilots, and as a working compromise the CAA's own Concorde test pilot Jock Reid joined British Airways captain Mike Bannister to carry out the taxi and flying tests on behalf of Airbus UK. The taxi trials went according to plan with the exception that one of the four Olympus powerplants gave cause for concern. But British Airways had no intention of compromising these vital proving trial flights and replaced the suspect engine with a recently overhauled unit.

Finally, on July 17 Concorde G-BOAF departed Heathrow on a test flight that would terminate at RAF Brize Norton in Oxfordshire. Once again Mike Bannister and John Reid were at the controls with five engineers on board to monitor the performance during the flight.

During a brief trip around Iceland, they took her up to 60,000 feet and through the sound barrier to Mach 1, before returning to Brize Norton. During this flight lasting just over three hours, the primary focus of attention would be whether or not the inclusion of the Kevlar linings within the fuel tanks would affect Concorde's complicated and vital fuel management systems throughout the flight. The day's events were heavily covered by the media, and both the departure from Heathrow and the arrival at Brize Norton were witnessed by thousands of airport workers and public spectators.

During two days on the ground at Brize Norton, extensive post test flight evaluations and checks were carried out. These checks included running the fuel tanks dry. In the case of an aircraft, 'dry' means the point at which the fuel tanks can no longer supply the engines with fuel. At the point where the engines stop there will be an amount of 'unusable fuel'

in the tanks. The purpose of the exercise is to determine the precise amount of usable fuel from full tanks. On the third day Concorde was fully checked and ready to make her return journey to Heathrow, following the same route via Iceland that she had flown three days before. All of the in-flight tests were repeated on the return leg to confirm the fact that

Concorde was now ready to go back into service.

As Concorde arrived back at London Heathrow the relief and optimism among engineers, pilots, management and everyone else who was involved with Concorde was at its highest for a very long time. However, as with all things within aviation, the road back into service still had a way to run. ■

▲ *An unusual view of Concorde arriving at the massive British Airways Heathrow engineering base for periodic servicing.*

Chapter 8

Back in Service

Once Concorde had been upgraded and would almost certainly get a new Certificate of Airworthiness, albeit following lengthy deliberations with the Civil Aviation Authorities, it was time to focus on the day to day operation requirements in order to return Concorde to scheduled services.

One refurbished Concorde was not enough. At least four more aircraft would have to be upgraded quickly in order to meet the serviceability levels required to re-start the New York schedule. In addition to the modifications required for re-certification, British Airways were committed to refurbishing the cabin interiors. Last but not least, although the Concorde service engineers were more than ready for action due to the extensive work they had carried out over the preceding months, the same could not be said for the flight and cabin crews, who apart from Mike Banister had not flown

Concorde for a year.

British Airways got underway with the simultaneous upgrading of both G-BOAE and G-BOAG. In September, when the first two aircraft were due to be completed, the engineers would go straight on to carry out the upgrades to G-BOAC and G-BOAD. This would provide sufficient aircraft to resume the New York service. Concorde G-BOAA and G-BAOB were due to be restored to line service early in 2002.

In August 2001 the first Air France Concorde to be modified, F-BVFB, took to the air from Charles de Gaulle airport to commence her flight testing for re-certification. Air France needed only enough aircraft to serve their less frequent New York service and therefore were in less of a rush to get the work done. They would return just three aircraft to service, beginning with F-BTSB and F-BVFB simultaneously, followed by completing the work on F-BFVC.

Unlike more modern flight simulators, the Concorde flight training simulator, now 30 years old, was not able to deliver trained pilots directly into scheduled line service. Although an excellent simulator that replicated real Concorde flying very accurately and realistically, it was designed to bring pilots up to a standard that would need finishing off with a period of base training, flying the real aircraft. The pilot re-training programme was carefully devised and G-BOAF left Heathrow for a holiday at Shannon airport in the south of Ireland, where the base training of the Concorde crews was completed. Similarly, after completing simulator training in Paris, the Air France flight crews adjourned to an airfield east of Paris called Vatry airport in order to

◀ *Looking pristine in the new Chatham livery, 2001 saw Concorde B-BOAG successfully complete all of her test flights carrying the modifications installed since the Paris crash.*

▶ *Without compromising safety, it is essential to roll the aircraft in and out of engineering as quickly as possible as time spent on the ground is very costly.*

complete their post simulator base training.

Early in September 2001 the British Airways marketing machine began to re-market Concorde as the queen of the skies that she had been for nearly three decades, along with the message that she was even safer to fly than ever before. Complimentary invitations to be wined and dined at British Airways facilities were extended to a select few of Concorde's most regular patrons. It was at this time also, on September 5, 2001, that the French and British Civil Aviation Authorities restored Concorde's Certificate of Airworthiness. Along with the faith that had been demonstrated by British Airways and Air France ahead of certification by pressing ahead with all return to service modifications and re-training, news of the re-certification confirmed that Concorde would be back in service within weeks.

Before returning Concorde to service, British Airways decided to fly five pre-operational proving flights with passengers (lucky BA staff). All of the operational procedures used on scheduled services would be in place. The aircraft would board its passengers through a refurbished Concorde lounge in Terminal 4 at Heathrow. All support services would be in place, including a standby aircraft, and the ground staff would be able to practise their duties in a real life simulation of a scheduled departure. Three of the flights would be three-hour return trips over the Atlantic during which the full transatlantic meal service would be provided for passengers and crew. Two more flights were made on a return trip to New York (even luckier BA staff) giving the New York ground crews live

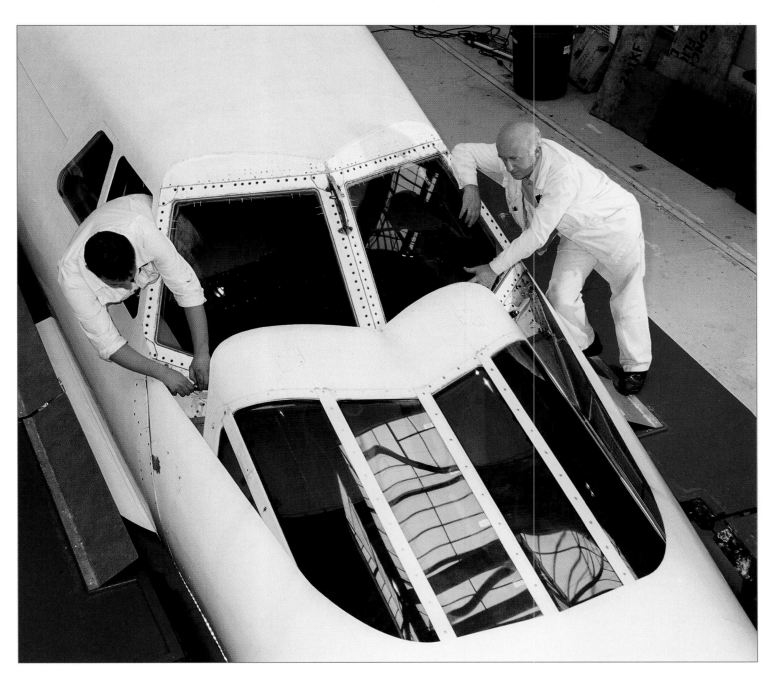

experience of handling the turn-around of the Concorde flight once more before services resumed.

NINE-ELEVEN

Then, an event occurred that would trigger Concorde's early demise. The terrorist attacks on the United States of September 11, 2001, which resulted in the tragic loss of thousands of lives, and involving the loss of four subsonic airliners. One of the proving flights took place at midday on Tuesday September 11, just as the news of the attack on the Twin Towers in New York was breaking to the British media.

This tragedy would have a direct impact on the future of Concorde. It had survived the early political and commercial assaults and struggled back from the aftermath of the Paris accident. Now many of Concorde's regular patrons had been killed and many more were now too frightened to fly at all. Once again, events that had nothing to do with Concorde herself were playing

▲ Being an elder of the fleet, every inch of Concorde, including her complex nose cone mechanisms, has to be examined for wear and tear or damage on a regular basis.

TIMELINE

October 1981

The British and French governments meet in London to review the future of Concorde. Unbelievably, all options are tabled, from total and immediate cancellation through gradual withdrawal from service, to indefinite support for Concorde operations. Both governments are keen to be free from the financial lifeline that they give to Concorde.

In March of this year US President Ronald Reagan was shot and wounded, in May Pope John Paul II suffers the same fate, and in June blank bullets are fired at the queen in London. In October, President Sadat of Egypt pays the price for promoting peace in the Middle East as he is gunned down and killed during a military parade in Cairo.

May 1982

Chairman of British Airways Sir John King forms a new division within British Airways tasked with taking on the full responsibility for profitability of Concorde operations.

At the beginning of April this year Argentina invaded and captured the British Falkland Islands. A massive British expeditionary force set sail for the Falklands in May and by the middle of June Argentina had surrendered, and British troops flew the Union Jack over Port Stanley. The following month, the IRA are still bombing London, with massive nail bombs planted in parked cars in Hyde Park and Regents Park. Eleven parading soldiers are killed and more than 75 people are injured.

August 1982

The British government informs British Airways that it is withdrawing Concorde-related financial support from British Aerospace (BAe) and Rolls-Royce.

Two more Hollywood stars die: first, Henry Fonda, followed later in the month by Ingrid Bergman.

October 1982

Sir John King informs the British government of a plan to meet Concorde support costs from revenue generated by the newly formed Concorde Division within British Airways. In France, the Air France Concorde operation is in trouble as the airline withdraws scheduled services between Paris and Washington.

Political change in Europe sees the socialist party taking power in Spain and Helmut Kohl becoming West German chancellor.

▶ *Opposite: The dreadful events in New York City on September 11th 2001.*

a significant part in her future.

Neither British Airways nor Air France wanted to make any public moves regarding Concorde in the aftermath of '9/11'. Both airlines had sufficient aircraft close to line readiness for scheduled services and would normally have been publicising a date for the resumption of services about this time. It was considered prudent to quietly press ahead with the completion of the first phase of fleet modifications and wait to see what impact '9/11' was having on the aviation world. Alpha Foxtrot would use the extra time by undergoing her 250 hours check, while work would be completed on G-BOAE and G-BOAG.

In France, Air France had been working closely with British Airways and the manufacturers and had two aircraft near to completion, F-BVFC and F-BTSD. In September Alpha Echo was rolled out of the hangars in readiness for her air tests. British Airways had contemplated the possibility that she might need more than one air test as she had been on the ground for a longer period than the rest of the fleet. This was because, prior to the withdrawal of the airworthiness certificates following the Paris crash, Alpha Echo had been grounded due to the discovery during a maintenance operation of minor cracks in one of her wing spars. Subsequently, these cracks were discovered on other aircraft in both the British and French fleets. A modification was devised to remedy the cracks and work was carried out on both fleets during the period that they were grounded.

By early November both Air France and British Airways would be ready to re-launch Concorde services to New York and, as had been the custom in the past, both airlines decided to re-start the services simultaneously on the same morning. In mid-October they

TIMELINE

January 1983
Around the seventh anniversary of Concorde in service, a British Airways Concorde re-sets the transatlantic crossing speed record by flying New York to London in just 2 hours and 56 minutes.

After a year of social struggle and martial law, Polish workers led by recently released Lech Walesa strengthen their position by forming unions. The world first woke up to the phenomenon of "Star Wars" in 1977 when George Lucas released the block buster movie – in March of this year Ronald Reagan talks about doing it for real.

Later this year, Margaret Thatcher is elected for a second term, a South Korean Jumbo Jet is shot down by Soviet fighters after straying into Soviet air space, and US-built cruise missiles start arriving in Britain.

March 1984
British Airways finally take on the responsibility of funding Concorde support services by British manufacturers out of British Airways' Concorde revenues.

In Britain the National Union of Coal Miners call an all out strike which will last twelve months. The following month, during demonstrations outside the Libyan embassy in London, woman PC Yvonne Fletcher is shot and killed by a gunman inside the embassy. Later in the summer Welsh-born actor Richard Burton dies.

September 1984
A British Airways Concorde sets a Concorde airborne distance record by flying 3,965 nautical miles between Washington and Nice.

Militants in Beirut drive a huge car bomb into the compound of the US embassy killing more than 20 people. Before the end of this year, the first woman has walked in space, Indian Prime Minister Indira Gandhi is assassinated, and Ronald Reagan wins a second term in the White House.

February 1985
Still hanging in there – a British Airways Concorde completes the first fare-paying Concorde charter between London and Sydney, covering the distance in just over 17 hours.

Still hanging in there – British Airways run a Concorde charter flight from London to Cape Town, completing the journey in just over eight hours.

Nelson Mandela is still in prison and resists attempts by the South African government to release him on their terms.

had made a joint announcement that scheduled services to New York would commence on November 7, with the flights departing Charles de Gaulle and Heathrow, respectively, at 10:30 in the morning. In fact, due to the one hour difference between the

Continental time clock and GMT, the Air France flight departed an hour earlier than the British Airways flight, at 09.30 GMT.

The difference in departure times was not that apparent when the aircraft arrived in New York. Air France's Concorde arrived to a rapturous welcome, with masses of airport workers and spectators cheering the flight's arrival. By the time the Air France passengers were in the lounge the British Airways Concorde was making her approach into New York's

▲ At 10.44 am on the morning of 7th November 2001 Concorde departs London Heathrow on her first scheduled return to New York after re-entering service.

▲ *During the months of inquest and investigation, modifications and testing – the aircrew of Concorde were constantly advised and trained to cope with the new element of terror permeating the world of aviation.*

JFK airport, and the cheering welcome was repeated.

The reaction in New York could not have been more different from that seen when the original New York services were announced nearly 30 years previously. The Mayor Rudolph Giuliani welcomed Concorde back and described her return as a business-as-usual confidence-building event, which was exactly the message that New York wanted to send to the rest of the world.

TIMELINE

April 1985
Still hanging in there – having been cannibalised for parts for some time, Concorde 214, G-BOAC, is rolled out by the Concorde Division of British Airways with a brand new interior re-fit and external livery.

Concorde G-BOAC breaks the 'in service' ground speed record by flying at 1,488mph.

South Africa continues to introduce reforms and repeal harsh legislation in an attempt to impress the majority black population and the rest of the world. This coming summer will see more bloodshed and terrorism around the globe in India, Sri Lanka and Lebanon. However, in Cambodia the horrific human slaughter by the Khmer

Rouge begins to retreat as its infamous leader Pol Pot steps aside. In September the wreck of the Titanic is found 73 years after she sank. As the year closes a volcanic eruption in Colombia and an earthquake in Mexico City claim the lives of nearly 50,000 people between them.

January 1986
On her tenth anniversary in service Concorde clocks up 71,000 hours of flying in excess of the speed of sound.

The US space programme celebrates and mourns this month: as deep space probe Voyager 2 arrives in close proximity to Uranus and begins to collect data, the shuttle Challenger explodes shortly after launch, killing all seven crew on board.

In the past, British Airways had always operated a policy where they would keep a spare aircraft, fully maintained in readiness in support of aircraft actually flying the route. Air France did not operate this policy. However, with the re-launch of the New York service and the fact that the aircraft had flown so few hours since their year-long layoff, both airlines were keen to have three aircraft each available. If they were to re-launch simultaneously whoever was ready first would have to wait for the other to complete.

British Airways were first to complete three aircraft modifications by rolling out G-BOAG and air testing her in October 2001. This was soon followed by a full dress rehearsal flight to New York. A few days later, Air France rolled out F-BVFC, the aircraft that had been stranded in New York when Concorde was grounded after the Paris crash. This was now the third Air France Concorde to receive the full modification programme. Shortly after, also in October, Air France carried out their own New York dress rehearsal flight. As with the British Airways flight, the Air France Concorde carried as passengers the engineers who had worked so hard during the previous year to put Concorde back

▲ *Concorde rolls-out on the runway at Heathrow after her first flight since re-entering service.*

TIMELINE

April 1986
The world gets a taste of nuclear disaster as a Russian nuclear power station in Chernobyl in the Ukraine pollutes Northern Europe with radioactive fall-out

July 1986
The British Prime Minister Margaret Thatcher goes supersonic for the first time by flying from London to Vancouver, Canada in Concorde.

Time for another royal wedding, this time Prince Charles's younger brother Prince Andrew marries Sarah Ferguson.

September 1987
Concorde sets a new record for the actual transatlantic distance between the coastlines of Newfoundland and Ireland; she completes the trip in one hour and thirty five minutes.

More terrorism, with more than 20 Jews killed while worshipping in a synagogue in Istanbul.

▶ *An unusual picture of a British Airways Concorde taking off from Chatreaux in France in 1998, another airfield used by the airline for training pupposes.*

in the air.

Ever nervous of anything going wrong, before restarting the schedule British Airways slotted in two further test flights in support of minor maintenance issues, and to provide yet more training for crews and ground staff.

No sooner was Concorde back in the air than cost implications began to loom. All of the world's airlines were experiencing depressed revenues following '9/11', and British Airways was no

TIMELINE

Oct/Nov 1987
Two records are set during these two months. First, British Airways carries passenger number 1,000,000 across the Atlantic, then land speed record holder Richard Noble completes one and a half transatlantic return trips in a single day – the first Concorde passenger to do so.

A fire breaks out beneath an aging wooden escalator at London's Kings Cross tube station. The fire engulfs the ticket office area and 30 commuters perish.

February 1988
The transatlantic speed record keeps coming down. A British Airways Concorde flies from New York to London in 2 hours 55 minutes and 15 seconds.

Celebrations continue as Australia commemorates the country's bicentenary and the landing of European settlers in January 1788. In the United Kingdom British merchant seamen are on strike and are joined by Britain's nurses in a day of action to protest over low pay.

exception. For this reason alone British Airways had implemented cost reduction measures across the airline. One of these cost savings – actually more to do with cash flow – would be that they would modify the remaining four aircraft in the fleet just one at a time rather than in pairs, as originally planned. However, they would keep a close eye on how air travel recovered and assess whether or not there still remained a market for two scheduled New York services per day. ▪

Chapter 9

The End of Concorde's Flying Career

Having been treated many times like a political football from her inception and throughout her 27 years in service, the year 2002 saw Concorde about to suffer once again from 'back room' dirty dealing. However, this time the dirty deed would not only have a commercial motivation but also a slightly nationalistic one – rather than the political motivations of the past.

Only this time around the outcome would bring Concorde's flying career to a close.

GET OUT QUICK

For many reasons Air France had never enjoyed the same level of commercial success that British Airways had achieved in operating their Concorde fleet. The Heathrow hub was strategically more viable for capturing premium ticket price flyers than Charles de Gaulle airport in Paris. Nor had Air France gone through the same 'renaissance' as British Airways had done during the early 1980s. The problems of funding and maintenance

responsibilities were a bigger issue for Air France due to continued government involvement and, of course, the Paris crash left many French airline and Airbus Industries strategists and planners wishing that they could walk quietly away from Concorde.

Behind the scenes, the desire to 'get out quick while the going was good' would have been a more accurate assessment of the feelings within Air France and Airbus.

Air France and the crash investigators examining the Paris accident knew only too well that maintenance errors and some poor judgement calls by the Air France crew probably contributed more to the crash than the final accident report would be prepared to admit. Indeed, such matters were kept very low profile in the final accident report, and also kept well clear of the media.

Perhaps the final straw was reached in early 2003 when a decision was made during a transatlantic flight to divert an Air France Concorde to Nova Scotia in order to carry out a precautionary landing. Once again, following an in-flight engine failure, not a particularly unusual or dangerous event, the Air France crew compromised the flight by mismanaging engine shut down procedures.

Having gone through the in-flight engine shut down checklist, the crew had overlooked the action of closing off the fuel supply to the dead engine. Again, this was not in itself too directly threatening, except for the fact that for ten minutes the aircraft was dumping large amounts of vital unused fuel reserves into the air over the Atlantic. The Air France Concorde was 'stranded' in mid-Atlantic with not enough fuel left on board to complete its journey to

TECHNICAL DATA

Concorde is fitted with two independent auto-pilots. During normal flight operations only one is used, with the other on ready stand-by. However, in the case of an automated landing, both autopilots would be on line, facilitating a live back-up in the case of a failure.

Concorde is fitted with three modes of auto-throttle control:
MACH HOLD – In the cruise this auto-throttle setting will control engine power to maintain selected Mach number for the cruise.
IAS HOLD – At any stage of the flight this mode will control engine power to maintain air speed to the airspeed selected by the crew.
IAS ACQ – In this mode, the crew can select the next required airspeed and the throttles will be automatically adjusted in order to acquire the selected airspeed; the system then reverts to **IAS HOLD**.

New York or to return to a European destination. Thankfully, the crew did have enough fuel for a diversion to Halifax, Nova Scotia, and landed with only minutes of flying time remaining. Once again the media failed to learn the truth behind the reasons for this diversion.

A DEAL IS DONE

All of this was too much for Air France, who now needed to withdraw their Concorde fleet from service even if it meant suffering the humiliation of seeing the refitted British Airways Concorde fleet continuing to provide the world's only supersonic passenger services. At this point, another large French aerospace company came to the rescue of Air France. Airbus were reluctantly underpinning Concorde's scheduled services by providing, at a cost, the spares and maintenance support required by both the British Airways and Air France fleets. With no prospect remaining for building and selling new Concorde aircraft, and only a handful still flying, this was a far less than ideal situation for Airbus. They could well do with diverting their manpower resources and production facilities from any Concorde work and focus their resources on current and new projects that carried sales potential.

And so a deal was done. Airbus would cease providing Concorde operational support unless British Airways and Air France came up with extra millions of euros and sterling to fund it. Air France readily declined to pay up any extra cash on behalf of the French government, and it was left to British Airways either to fall in line or try to go it alone.

Despite British Airways succeeding to returning their Concorde fleet to

▲ *Concorde G-BOAC Commanded by Captain Les Brodie leaves Barbados for the very last time on 30th August 2003. She was the first Concorde to visit the island in 1977 when she arrived there to collect the Queen at the end of her Jubilee tour.*

service and profit, world events were closing in on the carefree habit of high expenditure on air travel. Rising costs in industry, reduced expense budgets and a global fear of terrorism, were leading inexorably to a commercial melt-down which was slowly taking its toll on what had become the airline's mainstay of standard and premium class air travel. Increasingly, the travelling public, including business class travellers, were choosing air travel only when necessary and with an increasing demand for cheaper seats.

Reluctantly, British Airways realised that they probably had little choice in

TECHNICAL DATA

NOSE AND VISOR POSITION OPTIONS:

POSITION 1: nose and visor fully retracted in up position; deployed during supersonic cruise and when parked.

POSITION 2: nose fully up, visor retracted into droop nose; used during short subsonic cruise and to gain access to the wind-screens.

POSITION 3: nose down 5 degrees and visor retracted; used for taxi-ing and takeoff.

POSITION 4: nose down at 12.5 degrees, visor retracted; used for landings and taxiing, raised to 5 degrees soon after landing to avoid accidental damage.

what action they could take. This was an opportunity to withdraw Concorde from service in a joint action with Air France and Airbus, while at the same time distributing the blame and shame between the three companies. So it came to pass that British Airways, Air France and Airbus jointly announced the retirement of Concorde from scheduled services, and the airlines named the dates for their respective final Concorde flights.

AND A DEAL UNDONE

Inevitably, the announcement to end Concorde's scheduled service career drew an outcry from many quarters. British Airways staff, who had flown and nurtured Concorde over the years, knew full well that Concorde had many years of useful flying remaining. If not on scheduled services, then certainly events such as high profile charters and public appearances at air shows etc would be in high demand. The British travelling and general public were up in arms also; they were certain that Concorde should keep flying and that someone should be prepared to meet the cost in order to preserve this finest example of British aviation heritage. They conveniently forgot that it was

TIMELINE

April 1988

Twelve years since going into service, Concorde aircraft begin to be assessed for wear and tear. Production aircraft 206, G-BOAA, has completed 12,000 flying hours and undergoes a comprehensive structural check. It is assessed that the airframe would see service well beyond the end of the 20th Century.

In July disaster strikes the Piper Alpha oil rig in the North Sea as it explodes and bursts into flames, killing more than 160 workers. Two trains collide as they approach Clapham Junction, London, during the morning rush hour; 36 people are killed. As Christmas approaches, 270 people are killed as a Pan Am Jumbo Jet bound for New York is blown out of the sky over Lockerbie, Scotland by a terrorist bomb.

March 1989

Unbelievably, it is now 20 years since Concorde 001 made her maiden flight from the runway at Toulouse back in 1969.

The beginning of 1989 witnessed changes in two of the world's most powerful leaderships; in the USA George Bush senior is sworn in as America's 41st president, and Emperor Hirohito of Japan dies.

April 1989

During a 38,000-mile circumnavigation of the globe Concorde suffers a structural failure when she loses a section of the rudder in flight. This was to be the first of numerous rudder section losses experienced by Concorde.

Once again the New York to London record is broken. A British Airways Concorde reduces the time to 2 hours 54 minutes and 30 seconds.

As the year closes millions of people in Europe are freed from the grip of Soviet-imposed communism symbolised by the physical dismantling of the Berlin wall by the people of East and West Germany.

May 1990

Concorde enjoys a renewed and successful phase in her career: British Aerospace and Aerospatiale are talking openly about a successor to Concorde and British Airways are listening with a genuine high degree of interest.

Earlier this year storms rampage across the United Kingdom killing nearly 40 people. South Africa ends apartheid, and the British authorities intercept a 'super gun' about to be shipped to Saddam Hussein's Iraqi regime.

June 1990

This month sees the 50th anniversary of the 'Battle of Britain'. Concorde teams up with a World War II Spitfire and flies in formation with her over the 'White Cliffs of Dover'.

also a part of French aviation heritage.

Richard Branson, boss of Virgin Atlantic, threw his hat and his cheque book into the ring in an attempt to face down British Airways and transfer scheduled supersonic routes from British Airways to Virgin Atlantic.

The Civil Aviation Authority and the government in Britain knew that the Airbus decision to withdraw certification support for Concorde at a reasonable price was against the European Union's

TECHNICAL DATA

FUEL SYSTEM FUNCTION

Fuel tanks – numbers:
1,2,3 and 4
Fuel management task
Supply tanks to engines
Total fuel capacity
22,140ltrs (4,876 gals)
Total weight of fuel
38,579lb (17,536kg)

Fuel tanks – numbers:
5,6,7 and 8
Fuel management task
Main storage tanks
Total fuel capacity
49,280ltrs (10,854 gals)
Total weight of fuel
85,866lb (39,030kg)

Fuel tanks – numbers:
5A and 7A
Fuel management task
Auxiliary tanks
Total fuel capacity
5,620ltrs (1,238 gals)
Total weight of fuel
9,790lb (4,450kg)

Fuel tanks – numbers:
9, 10 and 11
Fuel management task
Transfer and reserve tanks
Total fuel capacity
42,240ltrs (9,304 gals)
Total weight of fuel
73,599lb (33,454kg)

ABOVE & LEFT: *After being mothballed for so long after the Paris crash, most of the Concorde fleet needed cosmetic treatment to paintwork and interior cleaning – all this on top of the extensive engineering modifications.*

TIMELINE

September 1990
A small-scale model of Concorde is installed in the middle of the roundabout on the approach to the tunnel leading to Heathrow's main entrance.

Margaret Thatcher resigns after 12 long and often controversial years in office. She is succeeded by John Major.

May 1991
Britain's royals take to the air once more on Concorde, the queen and the Duke of Edinburgh fly supersonic from London to Washington.

The year had opened in January with the launch of 'Desert Storm' as Coalition air forces bombed Iraqi targets including Baghdad, neutralising the Iraqi air force. This was followed in February with the launch of the ground war by the allies; by the end of the month it was all over.

History repeats itself as former Indian Prime Minister Rajiv Gandhi, son of assassinated Indian Prime Minister Indira Gandhi, is himself killed by an assassin's bomb.

In June the latest Balkans War begins. Just two days after declaring its independence, Slovenia is invaded by Slobodan Milosevich's Yugoslavian troops. In August Beirut Islamic militants release Britain's John McCarthy after five years in captivity; this is followed by the release of fellow hostage Terry Waite in November. Also in November, Freddie Mercury, the lead singer of the rock band 'Queen', dies.

March 1992
Another Concorde rudder section loss, this time on a scheduled flight between Heathrow and New York.

After just six years of marriage, the Duke of York, Prince Andrew, and Lady Sarah Ferguson announce that they are to separate.

May 1992
The rudder failure two months earlier was the third such failure to be experienced by the British Airways Concorde fleet. British Airways respond by announcing the replacement of the complete rudder section on all of their Concorde aircraft.

The satirical magazine Punch closes down after 100 years of publication. By the end of 1992, thousands of British miners lose their jobs, the UK is forced to leave the ERM, and part of Windsor Castle is destroyed by a fire.

March 1993
Two children aged three and twelve are killed by an IRA bomb in Warrington, Cheshire; more than fifty people are injured; a month later the City of London is ripped apart by another IRA bomb.

rules on competitive advantage. It could have been challenged in the courts on many different points of European law, but, for a change, the British government failed to intervene.

Perhaps under pressure from the public outrage, British Airways had secretly embarked on a study to evaluate the potential for a new company, formed, funded and supported by multiple airlines from around the world, to maintain the Concorde fleet and offer

TECHNICAL DATA

At Mach 2 Concorde's 'centre of lift' moves by six feet; this is compensated by transferring 20 tonnes of fuel to the rear trim tank. This is also done prior to takeoff when a rearward centre of gravity is preferable. The forward and rear trim tanks can move around 33 tonnes of fuel in order to maintain the correct centre of gravity during flight.

After landing fuel is transferred to the forward trim tanks to ensure that Concorde does not tip backwards onto the tail skid.

MAIN UNDERCARRIAGE:
Number of wheels each side, 4
      Operated by hydraulics
      Retracted inwards
Emergency operation:
      A – hydraulically lowered
      by standby system
      B – mechanical release and
      freefall to lock
Track 25 feet 4 ins. (7.72m)
      Tyre size 47x15.75-22
      Tyre type Michelin NZG
      External diameter 43.31 ins.
(110cm)
      Width 15.75 inches (40cm)
      Weight 176.4lb (80kg)
Max speed 280mph
      Tyre pressure 232psi
Brakes:
      4 sets of Dunlop carbon fibre
      callipers with anti-skid system

TIMELINE

March 1993
As British Airways and most of the world's airlines begin to promote more women pilots within their flying crews, Concorde welcomed her first female Senior First Officer, Barbara Harmer.

May 1993
British Airways embark on a one-million-pound internal and external refurbishment programme on their Concorde fleet.

November 1993
Concorde 206, G-BOAA, hits the headlines again by becoming the first of the British Airways Concorde fleet to receive the new rudder modification.

Soldiers are killed in Somalia after two US Black Hawk helicopters are shot down with rocket-propelled grenades. In Britain potential for real peace in Northern Ireland looms with the revelation that the British government have responded to requests for talks by the IRA.

October 1994
This month sees several commercial decisions heralding the fate of Concorde. British Airways withdraws the scheduled Concorde service between London and Washington. An additional aircraft is based in New York serving an increase in US-based Concorde charters. Back in the UK, Richard Branson is negotiating with the French on a plan to lease all of the Air France Concorde fleet and its crews.

In March the European Jet Fighter (later to be named Typhoon) makes her maiden flight. In May Brazilian F1 racing legend Ayrton Senna is killed during the San Marino Grand Prix in Italy. By year end Nelson Mandela becomes the first black South African president. Tony Blair becomes Labour leader, and Russia invades Chechnya.

May 1995
The man most individually described as the British Concorde designer was Sir Archibald Russell, CBE FRS. Sir Archibald died on May 29th.

America is gripped by panic following the terrorist bomb that ripped through a government building in Oklahoma killing more than 80 people.

September 1995
The Rolls-Royce Olympus 593 engine fitted to production Concordes has now logged more than 500,000 flying hours. Also this month, a double celebration for Europe: the European Ryder Cup golf team have won the trophy and are flown home in style in the world's only Supersonic Passenger Transport in service.

Before year end Israeli Prime Minister Yitzak Rabin is assassinated, and there is peace in the Balkans.

◀ *Concorde's first female First Officer – Captain Barbra Harmer.*

▼ *The very last Concorde landing at Heathrow in October 2003.*

supersonic charter flights well into the 21st Century. Having observed the incredible upsurge of public interest and demand for passenger bookings as Concorde approached the end of her scheduled services, this project was unquestionably viable. The plan was that the new company would get a kick-start by inheriting the British Airways Concorde fleet plus any stock-piles of spares that were available, free of charge.

Sadly, it was not to be. Airbus hardened its position and now refused to

support Concorde airworthiness certification at any price. Once again, the CAA and the British government refused to take up their options to launch a challenge in the courts. It is laudable that British Airways had made extraordinary efforts to keep Concorde in the air following the Paris crash. It was commendable that they were now working hard in secret to come up with a plan that would keep Concorde flying. However, they cannot escape a share of the blame, along with Airbus treachery, for terminating Concorde's passenger-

TECHNICAL DATA

NOSE GEAR:

Number of wheels, 2
    Operated by hydraulics
    Retraction direction, forwards
Emergency operation:
    A – hydraulically lowered
    by standby system
    B – mechanical release
    and freefall to lock
Tyre type:
    Dunlop (British Airways)
    Goodyear (Air France)
    Tyre size 31x10.75-14
    Tyre pressure 190psi
Brakes: None
Steering:
    Electrically signalled and
    hydraulically operated
    Maximum steering
    angle +/- 60 degrees

REAR TAIL PROTECTION WHEEL:
Number of wheels, 2
    Operated by hydraulics
    Retraction direction, rearwards
Emergency operation:
    None
    Tyre size 3.2x120-4.5-14
    Tyre pressure 294psi
Brakes: None

TIMELINE

January 1996
It is now 20 years since Concorde first entered service.

February 1996
As expected, Concorde is cleared to receive a life extension programme; this is not unusual for modern aircraft. What is unusual, if not amazing, is that the report ruled Concorde would not need any modifications and would require only half a dozen changes to her maintenance schedules. The New York to London record goes again, this time in just 2 hours 52 minutes and 59 seconds.

After a 17-month ceasefire the IRA return to bombing London with a massive blast in London's refurbished Docklands area. One month later at Dunblane in Scotland, a gunman walks into a primary school just after the start of classes and shoots dead 16 school children between the ages of five and six years old and wounds 12 more; the gunman then shoots himself. Four months later another man attacks staff and children with a machete at a nursery school in Wolverhampton, England; mercifully no one is killed.

June 1996
Passengers have been flying from Hounslow Heath for 50 years, albeit from assembling in the early days in canvas tents and setting off around Europe in aircraft that could only navigate by following railway lines and other land features. Now named Heathrow Airport and sporting four impressive terminals, Heathrow celebrates her 50th anniversary. To mark the occasion, Concorde teams up with yet another Royal Air Force warbird, the BAE Hawk. Concorde and the bright red Hawks of the Royal Airforce aerobatic display team, the 'Red Arrows', perform a low level flypast in formation over Heathrow airport.

The IRA strike again; there have been five other attacks since the Docklands bombing but a huge explosion shatters the Manchester city centre; there are hundreds of injuries but no one is killed.

August 1996
In 1907, just four years after the Wright brothers flew the world's first powered controlled manned aircraft, Sir Frank Whittle (*pictured inset above right*) was born and went on to invent the jet engine without which supersonic flight would never have been achieved. Sir Frank dies on August 8, 1996.

Once again, America is reeling from a terrorist bomb attack: at the Atlanta Olympics the previous month, two people were killed and scores more injured.

In October following the massacre in Dunblane, ownership of handguns is banned in the UK and the man who carried out the machete attack in July is found guilty and sentenced to life imprisonment.

◄ Opposite: Sir Frank Whittle (1907– 1996) the inventor of the jet engine who made supersonic flight a viable proposition.

carrying career. British Airways must in hindsight put up their hands for being, publically at least, a little indifferent and insufficiently supportive of continued Concorde services during the first half of 2003. So it was that the momentum for total cancellation of Concorde passenger services was able

to swiftly overrun any and all attempts to save supersonic passenger transport in the foreseeable future.

When the last passenger-carrying Concorde landed at London's Heathrow airport in October 2003 it brought supersonic passenger travel to an end. After nearly 10 years of development, followed by 25 years in passenger- carrying service, the era of SST was over.

For many, the retirement of such an advanced and unique aircraft seemed unbelievable and unacceptable. Many

▼ There were many occasions when Concorde would star at air shows around the world, teaming up with the Red Arrows for an exhilarating display, most notably though, and with the biggest audiences, were along The Mall and over Buckingham Palace to celebrate the Queen's Golden Jubilee and again to celebrate the Centenary of Heathrow Airport.

TIMELINE

January 1997
It is Concorde's 21st birthday in service and British Airways gives the fleet a new livery in line with a new 'British Airways Corporate Identity'.

This year Diana Princess of Wales was killed in a car crash in Paris.

July 1998
On July 25, 2000, a total of 113 people lose their lives as Air France Concorde F-BTSC crashes onto a hotel on the outskirts of Paris; four who die are hotel workers killed on the ground by falling wreckage.

August 2000
As Concorde G-BOAC makes her way along the Heathrow taxiways for a departure to New York, news comes that as a result of the Paris crash the Civil Aviation Authority is about to withdraw Concorde's Certificate of Airworthiness. G-BOAC is ordered to turn around and taxi back to the stand; Concorde operations are suspended. The next day both the British and French Concordes lose their certificates.

December 2000
By now it is confirmed that a burst tyre caused by debris on the runway at Charles de Gaulle airport, leading to the rupture of Concorde's fuel tanks, was the primary event which led to the Air France Concorde crash. The French crash investigators issue an interim report to that effect on December 12, 2000.

April 2001
Work is well under way to get Concorde back into the air. New tyres developed specially for Concorde by Michelin are being tested in France.

June 2001
Michelin are able to announce that their new tyres are a success and that they will be fitted to all Concordes on return to service.

April 2001
Work is under way to get Concorde back into the air. New tyres specially developed for Concorde by Michelin are being tested in France.

June 2001
Michelin are able to announce that their new tyres are a success and that they will be fitted to all Concordes on return to service.

July 2001
British Airways Concorde G-BOAF is modified and ready to embark on supersonic testing. She has the new tyres, fuel tank linings and enhanced protection against electrical fires. The test flight is successful, requiring no further modifications. One year after the Paris tragedy a memorial service is held in Paris for those killed in the accident.

▲ On October 24th 2003 all along the approach flight path into London Heathrow Airport, thousands of loyal spectators watched as three Concordes came home and made consecutive landings, taxiing along with flags flying to mark the sad end of their illustrious flying career.

TIMELINE

September 2001
September 11, 2001. Four American airliners are hijacked in the United States – the terrorists taking over the controls. Two aircraft crash into the World Trade Centre, destroying them completely, one crashes into the Pentagon in Washington, D.C., causing massive damage, and the fourth crashes into a field in Pennsylvania. All in all more than 2,600 are confirmed dead. The estimated real total loss of life approaches 3,000 souls.

October 2001
Concorde tickets go on sale again with the first flights to New York scheduled by British Airways and Air France for November 7, 2001.

December 2001
As 2002 approaches, to celebrate Concorde's return to service British Airways offer Concorde seats at a reduced price of £2,002. The booking lines close in less than four minutes, with all tickets sold. Concorde is back.

January 2002
The French accident investigators publish their final report on the Paris accident. There is nothing significantly new in their assessment of the causes of the crash. Many feel that there is scant reference to a range of Air France operational shortcomings that also contributed to the crash.

July 2002
G-BOAC is back in the air with a new Certificate of Airworthiness.

August 2002
It is 25 years to the day that the third Concorde prototype 101 or G-AXDN retired and made its last final approach and landing at Duxford airport to take up the role of static exhibit at the Duxford aircraft museum.

November 2002
It is another 25th anniversary: Concorde has been flying scheduled services from Paris and London to New York since 1977.

February 2003
Fears are raised again when an Air France Concorde has to be diverted to Halifax in Nova Scotia after reporting a fuel leak from an engine shut down over the Atlantic following an engine failure.

April 2003
British Airways, Air France and Aérospatiale jointly announce that Concorde is to retire from service, with the final flight in October 2003.

May 2003
Air France ends Concorde passenger services.

June 2003
Air France ends all Concorde flying operations.

October 2003
Three British Airways Concordes carry the last Concorde passengers into Heathrow airport.

pundits and the public believed that 'they' – the faceless industry moguls and their governments – would never really let it happen. But happen it did and, despite many theories suggesting political and commercial skulduggery, British Airways' explanation for

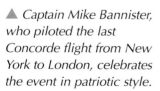 *Captain Mike Bannister, who piloted the last Concorde flight from New York to London, celebrates the event in patriotic style.*

Concorde's retirement may well stand the inevitable retrospective historical judgements of the future.

Despite overcoming development cost debts and moving into acceptable profit, particularly through the late 1980s and 1990s, even Concorde could not survive the shock wave created on September 11, 2001. In the aftermath of those tragic events, passenger travel and, in particular, the premium airline ticket market declined to levels where

only the fittest and most efficient of airlines could survive. Added to this was the fact that, after 30 years of flying, the Concorde production fleet was facing extensive and costly refit programmes in order to extend supersonic passenger travel into the 21st Century.

First class subsonic travel was a safer commercial bet requiring only changes to cabin configurations within existing fleets, rather than the sustaining of a completely separate aircraft type

designed to provide premium travel options. British Airways were producing dire estimates that investment in Concorde refits could lose £100 million over the next five to ten years if the premium airline ticket market did not significantly improve from its 2003 position.

Of the 20 aircraft that were built, the five development aircraft are already on static display in museums. One aircraft is in store under offer to the Brooklands aircraft museum. Concorde F-BVFD (production number 211) ended service in 1982 and was finally broken for spares in 1994. And, sadly, Concorde F-BTSC (production number 203) was lost in the Paris air crash on July 25, 2000. The remaining 12 aircraft have been allocated to museums around the world.

Details of the Concorde retirement homes are described in the final chapter of this book. ■

▲ *An earlier moment of glory saw British Airways put four Concordes into the air to be pictured flying in formation to celebrate the launch of the Chatham livery.*

Chapter 10

The Concordes –
and where are they now?

This book chronicles a long and sometimes sad tale of an aviation masterpiece that was and continues to be the people's aeroplane. Consistently compromised by decisions made behind closed doors, along dark corridors of power, the arguments surrounding her withdrawal from scheduled service will rumble on for decades. However, despite the tragedy that not a single Concorde is ever likely to take to the air again, all but three Concordes will remain accessible to the public. Seven aircraft will go on static display at airports in France, the United Kingdom and Barbados. The remaining ten aircraft will go to various museums in France, the United Kingdom, Germany and America, where it is hoped that the public will once again be able to enjoy close-up 'touch and feel' access to the queen of the skies.

Concorde 001 F-WTSS

Concorde 002 G-BSST

Concorde 101 G-AXDN

Concorde 102 F-WTSA

Concorde 201 F-WTSB

Concorde 202 G-BBDG

Concorde 203 F-BTSC

Concorde 204 G-BOAC

Concorde 205 F-BVFA

Concorde 206 G-BOAA

Concorde 207 F-BVFB

Concorde 208 G-BOAB

Concorde 209 F-BVFC

Concorde 210 G-BOAD

Concorde 211 F-BVFD

Concorde 212 G-BOAE

Concorde 213 F-BTSD

Concorde 214 G-BOAG

Concorde 215 F-BVFF

Concorde 216 G-BOAF

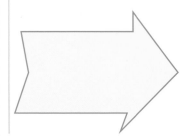

Concorde 001 F-WTSS

Concorde 001 (*pictured below*) was the first prototype and the first ever Concorde to fly. Owned by the Sud Aviation/British Aircraft Corporation (BAC) consortium, she first flew in March 1969 and accumulated a total of 812 flying hours. She is now preserved in the Air and Space Museum at Le Bourget airport, in Paris. ■

Concorde 002 G-BSST

Concorde 002 (*pictured below*) was the second prototype. Owned by the Sud Aviation/British Aircraft Corporation (BAC) consortium, she first flew in April 1969 and accumulated a total of 836 flying hours. She is now preserved in the Royal Naval Aircraft Museum at Yeovilton in Somerset. ■

Concorde 101 G-AXDN

Concorde 101 (*pictured below*) was the first pre-production aircraft. Owned by the Aérospatiale /British Aircraft Corporation (BAC) consortium, she first flew in December 1971 and accumulated a total of 633 flying hours. She is now preserved in the Imperial War Museum at Duxford in Cambridgeshire. ∎

Concorde 102 F-WTSA

Pre-production Concorde 102 or '02' was the second of two pre-production aircraft to be built, and carried nearly all of the full production specification of the production fleet. Dedicated to a pre-production development role, she was owned by BAC/Aérospatiale and first flew in January 1973, accumulating a total of 656 flying hours. These developments included a reshaped wing, redesigned tail cone, the latest air intake design for the Olympus 593, and the thrust reverse system.

In 1973 she carried more than 30 invited guests as passengers on her first visit to the United States of America. Even on these early flights, the Atlantic flight time between Dallas and Paris was only just over three-and-a-half hours. The transatlantic flight time record was broken many times during Concorde's flying career, and these early flights were not far short of the ultimate records set by the time that Concorde retired.

In 1976, after just 656 flying hours, Concorde 102, registered as F-WTSA, retired to static display at Orly airport where she replaced a model of Concorde that had been destroyed in a fire. The final months of her career after finishing test flying had been extensive taxi trials to certificate modifications to the braking systems, thrust reversers and undercarriage water deflectors.

The aircraft was cannibalised for engines and other spare parts to support the maintenance programme for Air France Concordes that were still in service. In return for this sad and ignominious end to a flying icon, as she was on show to the public, all of her test equipment was removed and she was fitted with an 'in service' cabin interior. Apart from the 1973 transatlantic flight referred to earlier, this would be the closest that she ever came again to welcoming passengers on board.

Disaster almost struck in 1988 when the Orly airport managers decided that the airport no longer needed the presence of the fourth Concorde airliner ever to be built and she came close to being dismantled for scrap. However, an organisation known as Athis-Paray-Aviation came to her rescue and she was moved to a new display stand at the Museum Delta in Athis-Mons, outside the perimeters of Orly airport. ■

Concorde 201 F-WTSB
Concorde 201 was the first production test aircraft. Owned by the Aérospatiale /British Aircraft Corporation (BAC) consortium she first flew in December 1973 and accumulated a total of 909 flying hours. She is now on static display outside of the Aérospatiale headquarters in Toulouse. ■

Concorde 202 G-BBDG
Concorde 202 (*pictured opposite*) was the second production test aircraft. Owned by Aérospatiale /British Aircraft Corporation (BAC) consortium she first flew in February 1974 and accumulated a total of 1,282 flying hours. She is now at Brooklands Museum, Weybridge, Surrey, where she awaits funding for a complete restoration to static display.

Concorde 202 carried on flying after the 14 production aircraft had been delivered to the airlines. Work included further performance enhancements, such as the certification of the re-designed air intake profile. This modification, coupled to an uprated engine, allowed an increase in payload of 1,500-2,000lb.

Another change was an extension of the control surface trailing edges (by around two inches) – a modification that many now feel was part of the reason for the rudder de-laminations seen on the fleet over the years.

The aircraft was kept serviceable at Filton throughout early 1982 for any development work or test flights that were required.

At the end of the Concorde project the aircraft was placed in storage out on the airfield. British Airways were given access, through their support contract, to use the aircraft for certain parts that were not immediately available. In April 1984 they acquired title to the aircraft and started using it as one of the main spare part sources. The airline had been flying only six aircraft and had been using a four-year-old aircraft, G-BOAG, for spares. With access to Delta-Golf, British Airways set out to return G-BOAG to flight status.

To protect their investment, and to keep prying eyes off what was quickly becoming an eyesore, British Airways built a special hangar for G-BBDG, affectionately called the '202 hangar', and completed in early 1988. The aircraft, minus its tailfin, was moved inside in May 1988.

As the aircraft was structurally sound, British Airways investigated, in the early 1990s, the possibility of refitting her for airline service. This would allow the airline to keep a fleet of six or seven serviceable aircraft during engineering checks. The plan was found to be too costly and was rejected. However, the study proved that if one of the seven BA aircraft suffered serious damage, parts from the damaged (and written off) aircraft could be fitted to 202 and the airframe used to bring the fleet back up to strength. But there were doubts on certification, due to the fuselage skin being slightly thinner.

In 1995, G-BOAF's nose was damaged during an incident at Heathrow. BA decided to swap it for the nose on 202. Alpha-Foxtrot's nose, although not badly damaged, was kept as a spare and would be repaired if required. It was not put back onto 202.

Even as it looked like the end of the road for Delta-Golf, she was again found to be useful in late 2002 for prototype fittings of the new strengthened cockpit doors that had to be installed on the BA and AF fleets following September 11, 2001. ■

Concorde 203 F-BTSC

Concorde 203 (*see below*) was delivered to Air France and she first flew in January 1975, accumulating a total of 11,989 flying hours. Sadly, she crashed on takeoff from Paris Charles de Gaulle airport in 2000 with the loss of all passengers and crew on board plus casualties on the ground. The debris recovered from the crash site remains in storage in a hangar at Le Bourget airport. ■

Concorde 204 G-BOAC

Concorde 204 was delivered to British Airways and she first flew in February 1975, accumulating a total of 22,260 flying hours. She is now on display at Manchester airport in the UK. ■

Concorde 205 F-BVFA

Concorde 205 was delivered to Air France and she first flew in October 1975, accumulating a total of 17,824 flying hours. She is now on display at the Smithsonian's air museum at Dulles International airport, Washington, USA. ■

▲ *Concorde 206 G-BOAA, loaded on to a barge for her trip down the River Thames and then on to Scotland. She sits high and dry as she waits for the incoming tide at Syon Park, Isleworth.*

▶ *The huge barge completely blocks off the backwater running behind the famous 'London Apprentice' public house.*

Concorde 206 G-BOAA

Concorde 206 (*see above*) was delivered to British Airways and she first flew in November 1975, and accumulated a total of 22,786 flying hours. She is now on display at Edinburgh's East Fortune airport in Scotland. ■

Concorde 207 F-BVFB

Concorde 207 was delivered to Air France and she first flew in March 1976, accumulating a total of 14,771 flying hours. She is now on display at Sinsheim Auto and Technic Museum in Germany. ■

Concorde 208 G-BOAB

Concorde 208 was delivered to the British Aircraft Corporation and then re-registered to British Airways. She first flew in May 1976 and accumulated a total of 22,297 flying hours. She is now parked close to the threshold of runway 27 Right at Heathrow airport, and will soon take up a permanent static display position at Heathrow. ■

Concorde 209 F-BVFC

Concorde 209 was delivered to Air France and she first flew in July 1976, accumulating a total of 14,332 flying hours. She is now stored at the Airbus factory in Toulouse, France.

Concorde 210 G-BOAD

Concorde 210 was delivered to the British Aircraft Corporation and then re-registered to British Airways. First flown in August 1976 she accumulated a total of 23,397 flying hours. She is now displayed at the Intrepid Air and Space Museum in New York. ■

Concorde 211 F-BVFD

Concorde 211 was delivered to Air France and she first flew in February 1977, accumulating a total of 5,821 flying hours. Having been withdrawn from service in 1982 she was finally dismantled in 1994. Some remains of the main hull are in storage in a hangar at Le Bourget airport. ■

Concorde 212 G-BOAE

Concorde 212 was delivered to the British Aircraft Corporation and then re-registered to British Airways. She first flew in March 1977 and accumulated a total of 23,376 flying hours. She is now on static display at Grantly Adams airport in Barbados. ■

Concorde 213 F-BTSD

Concorde 213 was delivered to Air France and she first flew in June 1978, accumulating a total of 12,974 flying hours. She is on static display at the Le Bourget Air and Space Museum in Paris.

Concorde 214 G-BOAG

Concorde 214 (*pictured below*) was delivered to the British Aircraft Corporation and then re-registered to British Airways. She first flew in April 1978 accumulating a total of 16,239 flying hours. She is now on display at the Museum of Flight in Seattle, USA. ■

Concorde 215 F-BVFF

Concorde 215 was delivered to Air France and she first flew in December 1978, accumulating a total of 12,420 flying hours. This aircraft remains in the ownership of Air France and is scheduled to go on display at Charles de Gaulle airport in Paris. ■

Concorde 216 G-BOAF

Concorde 216 was initially delivered to the British Aircraft Corporation and consequently re-registered to British Airways. She first flew in April 1979 and accumulated a total of 18,275 flying hours. She is currently in storage at the Airbus factory in Filton near Bristol, and it is hoped that she will go on static display at a new aviation museum at Filton airport. ■

Appendix 1

Catering for Concorde's Passengers

ABOVE: *One of the delights of dining aboard Concorde was always the freshness and superb quality of the produce used in the preparation of the dishes.*

ABOVE RIGHT: *A typical Concorde menu.*

RIGHT: *One of the British Airways supply service units re-stocks Concorde between flights.*

LEFT: *The land-based kitchens servicing Concorde exercised the very finest standards of preparation and hygiene.*

ABOVE: *A typical Concorde passenger's place setting.*

BELOW: *The British Airways supply service staff who attended to Concorde's needs between flights.*

Appendix 2

The Uniforms of Concorde's Flight Crew

The criteria for Concorde aircrew and flight service staff was always to be of the highest quality. Staff, whether aircrew or cabin, were selected on the basis of their ability to perform their duties professionally, efficiently, and in a friendly, yet unobstrusive manner.

And at all times they were expected to look smart and well turned out. The uniform design reflects this philosophy, being at the same time relaxed and casual yet retaining a crisp businesslike appeal.

It was regarded as a peak in professional standards to be rewarded by being chosen to work on Concorde.

Appendix 3

Concorde Ephemera

The printed ephemera designed for use with Concorde has always reflected its high standards and personal service, special tickets being issued to celebrate milestone events.

All the material was tightly co-ordinated in style and closely monitored to ensure that every element was both functional and discreetly sophisticated.

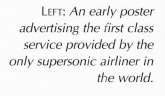

LEFT: An early poster advertising the first class service provided by the only supersonic airliner in the world.

BELOW: A selection of the various tickets, luggage labels and general ephemera of Concorde.

OPPOSITE BOTTOM: A selection of stationery, gift wallets and writing materials – all bearing the unmistakeable Concorde image of elegance.

Index

Figures in **bold** type indicate references in captions to illustrations.